WHERE TO FISH:
North-East
Stillwater Trout Fishing

Bob Smith & Alan Young

Published by Sigma Leisure – an imprint of
Sigma Press, 1 South Oak Lane, Wilmslow, Cheshire SK9 6AR, England.

British Library Cataloguing in Publication Data
A CIP record for this book is available from the British Library.

ISBN: 1-85058-757-4

Typesetting and Design by: Sigma Press, Wilmslow, Cheshire.

Printed by: MFP Design & Print

Cover Design: Sid Richards

Map Design: Morag Perrott

Photographs: authors' own except where indicated

Acknowledgements

We would like to thank the managers and wardens of all the fisheries for their wholehearted support in supplying us with the detailed information we needed to write this book. In particular we would especially like to thank Mr. Paul Russell and Mr. Don Coe of Northumbrian Waters Leisure and Tourism department for their time and efforts to make statistical information and photographs available for all the reservoirs under their control.

We are also grateful to Mr. Peter Godfrey, Mr. Ian Fairgrieve, Mr. David Carrick and Mr. Neil Cowans for their contributions to other sections of the book. Special thanks also to Kate for translating our scribbles onto the computer.

Finally, we give our sincere thanks to the many anglers throughout the region whom we met over the years, talked to, fished with and have become firm friends.

Bob Smith and Alan Young

This book is dedicated to Janet and Christine, our long-suffering wives, who "allow" us to go fishing so often and for so long.

Contents

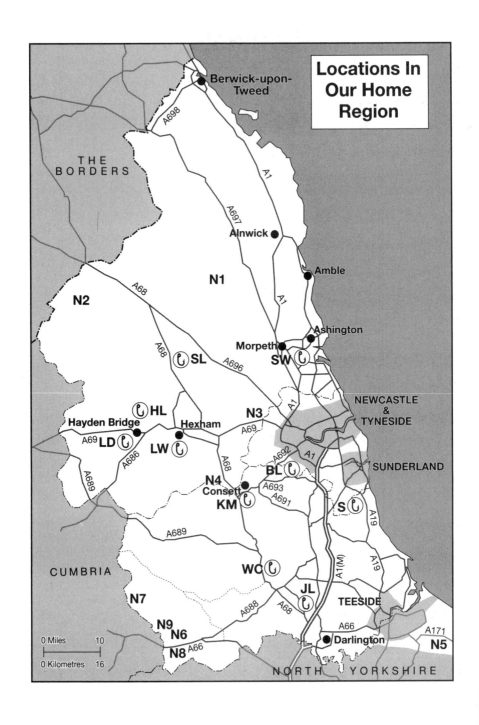

Locations In Our Home Region

Berwick-upon-Tweed

A698

THE BORDERS

A697

A1

Alnwick

Amble

N1

A68

N2

A1

A68

SL

Ashington

Morpeth

SW

A696

HL

N3

NEWCASTLE & TYNESIDE

Hayden Bridge

Hexham

A69

A68

A692

A1

SUNDERLAND

A69

LD

LW

BL

S

A686

N4

Consett

A693

KM

A691

A689

WC

A1(M)

A19

A19

CUMBRIA

N7

JL

TEESIDE

N9

N6

A688

A68

A66

0 Miles 10

N8 A66

Darlington

A171

0 Kilometres 16

N5

NORTH YORKSHIRE

Key to Map

Private Waters

BL   Beamish Lakes

HL   Harian Lodge

JL   Jubilee Lakes

KM   Knitsley Mill

LD   Langley Dam

LW   Linnel Wood Lakes

S   Sharpley Waters

SL   Sweethope Loughs

SW   Sleekburn Waters

WC   Witton Castle Lakes

Northumbrian Waters

N1   Fontburn Reservoir

N2   Kielder Water

N3   Whittle Dene

N4   Derwent Water

N5   Scaling Dam

N6   Hury Reservoir

N7   Cow Green Reservoir

N8   Blackton Reservoir

N9   Grassholme Reservoir

Introduction

This book offers information to anglers on the different venues that are available within the region: stillwaters ranging from a few acres in size to reservoirs of several hundred acres and larger. We have tried to cover our home region, which stretches from the Scottish border to the south of County Durham and west to the Pennine Hills.

All information has been gained from personal visits, or given by the fisheries themselves. Details are correct to the best of our knowledge at the time of print but: *We strongly recommend that anglers should telephone any fishery before visiting, to book a rod, confirm fishery rules and obtain ticket prices. Every fishery, to our knowledge, always has the time to make bookings and answer any questions or queries that anglers may have.*

All travel tips, with the individual fishery location maps, give what we feel to be the *easiest* route to the fishery. There may be shorter routes but they are probably more complicated. If unsure, please check with the fishery management when booking your day!

Please remember that before trout fishing anywhere, any angler

A fully finned Rainbow (6lb 12oz) caught in a Northumbrian fishery

aged twelve years and over who wishes to fish in England or Wales for salmon, trout, freshwater fish or eels, is required by law to have a current, valid Environment Agency Rod Licence (EARL) – these are obtainable from all Post Offices. If you fish without a licence you may be liable to prosecution. In addition to having an EARL, anglers also require a permit to fish from the fishery management before commencing to fish. Anglers must not discard any unwanted nylon anywhere as it is a death threat to numerous forms of wildlife. This is a vitally important point and must be observed at all times – anglers need to protect the environment to maintain a good image within society.

We feel it is important to keep fishing records and to try new venues. To help anglers do this we have included a "fishing log" which can be used at each fishery. Its use is described on page 101.

As mentioned in the book, some of the fisheries have *Troutmaster* status. This is a competition run by the national *Trout Fisherman* magazine. This competition requires anglers to catch one of the three heaviest fish each month from any Troutmaster water. Successful anglers receive a Troutmasters badge with logo and the year printed on it. At the end of the year the thirty-six lucky anglers (three per month), fish at the venue where they caught their heavy fish. The winner of this fish-off then represents that fishery in the Troutmasters final.

The latest information on the North-East stillwater trout scene can be gained from radio, local newspapers and magazines. The Newcastle local daily newspaper *The Journal*, and the evening edition, *The Evening Chronicle*, both carry weekly updates on "Game angling". Saturday's *Journal* carries a full page devoted to fishing under the heading, "The Reel Thing". Although there are articles on sea and coarse fishing, the game fishing section, written by George Macintyre, carries all the latest news from the region's stillwaters: the week's local scene, names of anglers, catches and venues. One interesting aspect of "The Reel Thing" is the "fly-box". The "fly-box" names the local venues and the successful flies of the week. Not all venues are always named, but should anyone be visiting a named fishery mentioned that week, they will have a good idea of what flies they need to carry.

Thursday night's *Evening Chronicle* has a full page trout fishing section called "Hooked" written by Sam Harris and David Carrick.

This keeps everyone up to date with the latest catches, forthcoming competitions, results, disabled anglers involvement with the sport and children's special events.

The **stillwater trout round-up** lists each venue from the region, plus some from Cumbria and southern Scotland, in alphabetical order and gives a brief outline of the week. For example, the Northumbrian Water Reservoirs sections lists the numbers of anglers that have fished that week, the number of trout caught, the total number of limit bags caught, the heaviest fish recorded and the weight of the best bag.

The **privately owned stillwaters** section gives the average number of fish caught per angler, the angler catching the best fish of the week (with its weight), best bag of trout and sometimes an outstanding number caught on the catch and release policy. Sometimes the weather is mentioned along with successful flies and tactics. In this section there is also a table of "Northern Stillwater Trout Form at a Glance". This names each fishery or reservoir, then proceeds to give the rod average for the week, the best trout that week, the best trout

Jack Charlton with disabled anglers *(Sharpley Waters)*

for the present season, the most successful fly for the week and a telephone contact number.

Another source of up-to-date information about trout fishing is local radio. "Howe's Fishing" programme is broadcast by Radio Newcastle (95.4, 104.4, 96.0 and 103.7 FM or 1458 metres AM) on Saturdays, 6.30-7.00am and on Sundays from 3.00-3.30pm.

A lot of work for the disabled angling scene in the North-East has been done by the Jack Charlton Disabled Anglers Trust. The Trust has organised a competition on Kielder Water for some years now. This is very popular, and around a hundred disabled anglers enter from all over Britain. Members of the Tyne and Wear Fly Fishing Association (TWFFA) do sterling work at the Kielder competition by providing the stewards and boatmen to help out. Winners of the Kielder championship then travel to Rutland Water to compete in the national finals. The top rods at Rutland then go on to represent England. There are also some disabled angling clubs who organise their own outings and competitions at a number of venues. One group regularly fishes Fontburn Reservoir near Rothbury in Northumberland.

More information about the National Disabled Fly Fishing scene can be gained from Derek Lucas who lives in Leicestershire and can be contacted on 0116 278 5485

Private Still Waters

Beamish Fly Fishery

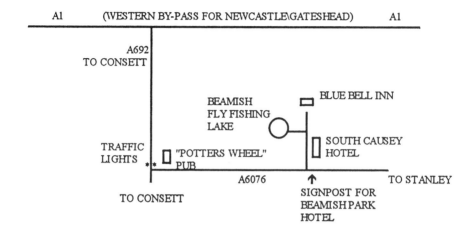

A1   (WESTERN BY-PASS FOR NEWCASTLE\GATESHEAD)   A1

A692
TO CONSETT

BEAMISH FLY FISHING LAKE

BLUE BELL INN

SOUTH CAUSEY HOTEL

TRAFFIC LIGHTS

"POTTERS WHEEL" PUB

A6076

TO STANLEY

TO CONSETT

SIGNPOST FOR BEAMISH PARK HOTEL

Travel tips: Leave the A1 western by-pass and take the A692 road to Consett. Continue on this road until the traffic lights at the "Potters Wheel" pub. Turn left at this junction towards Stanley on the A6076. Continue on this road until the signpost for Beamish Park Hotel. Turn left and continue past the railway down the hill and up the opposite side of the valley. Near the top of the climb and just before the Blue Bell Inn (on your left) is a narrow track which leads to the lakes, (be careful or you may miss it). Map not to scale.

As a trout-fishing venue, Beamish has improved tremendously over the last two years. As well as the main one and a half-acre fly fishing lake, there are also two worm-fishing lakes that are ideal for the beginner or for supervised children.

The fly fishing lake has some casting platforms and others are planned. The lake can take about sixteen rods and is now run by a syndicate. Beamish is a Troutmasters Water and also awards a monthly prize to the angler who catches the heaviest fish. This water mainly contains rainbow trout but there are some brown trout too. Rainbows are restocked weekly from two pounds up to double-figure fish. There are always about 450 fish in the lake, and this level is maintained throughout the year.

Tackle can be hired from the caravan and a selection of flies can be bought. A clean "porta-loo" plus soap and water are provided. Tea and coffee are freely available and meals and accommodation can be found in the nearby South Causey Hotel.

The lodge has comfortable seats, a television, a set of scales to weigh your fish, and a fridge to keep them in until you are ready to leave. Disabled anglers are welcomed and help is available if required.

The tickets available at Beamish fishery are:

➤ Keep three fish then catch and release

➤ Keep four fish then catch and release

➤ Four fish on worm

➤ Evening tickets (four hours)

These tickets require that anglers must kill their first two, three or four fish on their ticket and then they can catch and release a further eight fish. Children under the age of twelve fish on a parent's ticket.

The sessions at Beamish fishery vary from summer to winter. In winter the times are from 8am until dusk, while in summer anglers can fish from 7am until 4.30pm or 4.30pm until dusk. Evening tickets can be agreed by arrangement from May 1st.

Syndicate members who manage this fishery willingly give advice and have created a friendly, welcoming atmosphere.

Beamish worm lakes with fly lake in background

Hadrian Lodge

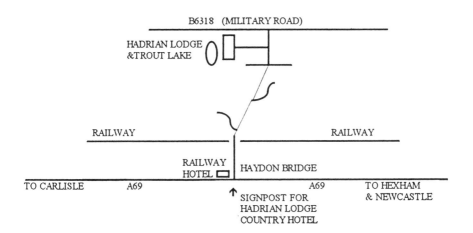

Travel tips: Journey to Haydon Bridge along the A69 which links Newcastle and Carlisle. Turn north in the village at the signpost for Hadrian Lodge Country Hotel. Follow this minor road up the steep hill (1:10) and keep on this road for 2-3 miles. Hadrian Lodge Hotel will be seen on your left. Map not to scale

Hadrian Lodge Hotel is found high on the north side of the Tyne Valley above Haydon Bridge. It is only two miles from the world famous Roman Wall, and the lake lies immediately to the west of the hotel building. The lake itself is about 150 metres long and 30 metres wide. The northern end of the lake is shallower and is covered with lily pads. This vegetation covers about a quarter of the lake.

The lake contains a few brown trout, but most are rainbows that are restocked when necessary with fish from one and a half pounds to three pounds. The fishery is open all year to residents from the hotel or visiting day anglers. The water can take up to six rods and anglers can fish from 7.30am until dusk. Payment for fishing is self-ticketing from a wooden hut between the hotel and the lake.

The Lodge will provide toilet facilities for anglers and bar meals are available between Easter and October. Sandwiches can be made at other times of the year if requested (by prior arrangement). The Hotel offers Bed and Breakfast and has five self-catering cottages. Anyone using these cottages can fish free at any time, but must pay for any fish they keep.

Visiting anglers have a choice of three tickets:

➤ keep first two fish, then catch and release

➤ keep first four fish, then catch and release

➤ an evening ticket

Once, when fishing here, I met a Mr Cook, who was staying at the Hotel, and was on holiday from Lincolnshire. Mr Cook thought this was an ideal situation because he was a keen fisherman. His typical day went something like this:

6.30am – 9.00am: trout fishing on the lake while the family slept.

9.00am – 6.00pm: away with his wife and family walking, visiting historical sites, or shopping at the Metro Centre in Gateshead, or in Newcastle, Carlise or Hexham.

6.00pm – dusk: return to Hadrian Lodge and fish for the rest of the day.

Hadrian Lodge is one of the smallest stillwaters in the area, but offers anglers a real challenge and as Mr Cook said, "It's ideal because the situation keeps me *and* my family happy when on holiday".

Hadrian Lodge *(courtesy of Hadrian Lodge)*

Jubilee Lakes

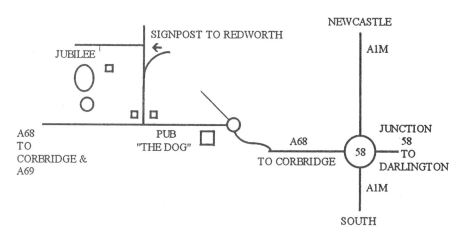

Travel tips: Travelling on the A1m, leave at junction 58 and follow the A68 for Corbridge. Pass "The Dog" public house and carry on to the top of the hill. Just after the brow of the hill turn right between the farm buildings. Follow the narrow road and take the first left just as the road bends to the right. Follow this road taking the first left again and Jubilee is on the left at the bottom of the bank, (look out for the large iron gates). Map not to scale.

Jubilee Lakes has a deserved reputation for being a first-class trout fishery that can compare very favourably with anything of a similar size in England. There are two lakes: the Lower Lake is two acres and has twelve feet of water at its deepest point. The Upper Lake is one acre and is around ten feet deep. Both lakes are fed by artesian well water and contain brown and rainbow trout. Rainbows are restocked daily and vary from two and a quarter pounds to twenty-five pounds. All of these fish are keen to do battle and will test any angler and their equipment to the limit.

Jubilee caters for the complete angler – it offers excellent fishing, a convenient car park, a shop, office, anglers' cabin and a toilet block. The whole complex is open throughout the year except on Mondays, Christmas Day and New Year's Day.

The car park is only yards from the Lower Lake, shop, toilets and anglers' cabin which is ideal for the disabled fishers. The stone-built buildings are immaculately clean and the anglers' cabin has a hot drinks machine, while hot snacks are available from the shop. The shop, known as "The Anglers' Lodge" is stocked with top-quality

Jubilee lower lake *(courtesy of Jubilee Lakes)*

tackle, clothing and fly tying materials. Everything is available by mail order and catalogues are updated in spring and autumn.

Sandra and Dave Hyman have owned the fishery since 1988 and have obviously worked hard to develop the fishery to the highest standards. Sandra and Dave also organise specialist days and courses throughout the year.

Anglers and beginners can hire rods and tackle if required and professional tuition can be arranged if requested. National River Authority licences can be bought from the Anglers Lodge if required.

Fishing begins at 8.30am until 8.30pm, or half an hour before sunset. Saturdays are slightly different, when fishing ends at 7pm at the latest. Day tickets are currently £10 plus £1.90 per lb of trout to a maximum of £5.95 per fish. Parent and Child tickets are available. A twenty-day season ticket can be bought too. When fishing, the first fish caught must be kept, then anglers can catch and release a further six fish from each lake. Any double-figure trout must be kept but will only cost £5.95. All brown trout must be returned.

There is a bank rotation system for all anglers. The smaller top lake has three sections of bank while the larger, lower lake has four sections of bank. The fishery policy allows anglers to fish any one stretch of bank for a maximum of two hours. After that, anglers must move to another section of bank, and may not return to the original section for at least two hours. This seems a very sensible policy as it helps all anglers to fish a number of areas throughout the day. It also prevents anyone fishing a particular spot for all that day. Some people like to cast with the wind behind them, so this prevents others from casting into the wind all the time. Moving around is good for everyone and appreciated by the vast majority of anglers, hence the popularity of Jubilee.

The record rainbow weighs 24lbs 10oz. The fisheries reputation has been further enhanced with anglers catching seven rainbows each weighing over 20lbs. Another 130 rainbows tipped the scales over 10lbs in weight.

Jubilee is a Troutmasters water and is always popular, so booking is essential. Anglers come from all over Britain in their quest for a double-figure fish so bed and breakfast can be arranged if requested.

Knitsley Mill

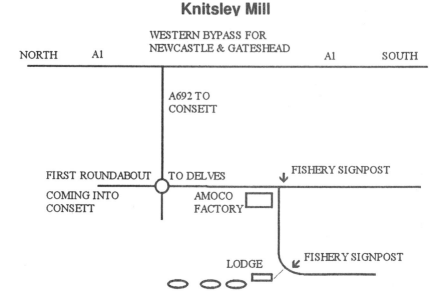

Travel tips: Leave the A1 western bypass and head for Consett on the A692. Keep on this road and as you enter Consett at the first roundabout turn left, (signposted for Delves). Continue along this road to the Amaco factory and turn right, (there is a fishery signpost at this junction). Continue down the hill and at the very bottom is the fishery entrance on your right. Map not to scale.

Knitsley Mill is found nestling in a quiet, picturesque, tree-lined valley near Consett. The fishery has three lakes that total five and a half acres. The lakes are brook- and spring-fed. The middle one, Oak Lake, is twelve feet deep in the middle and the newer, Lower Lake, is sixteen feet deep near the dam wall.

Both lakes are restocked daily with rainbows ranging from one and a half to two and a half pounds, but there are good numbers of larger fish including "doubles".

Waders are not required as fishing spaces are marked and there is a boat to hire. Tuition is available if requested in advance.

Knitsley is open throughout the year and fishing is from 8am until dusk. Three different tickets are available, each being catch-and-release:

➤ Full-day, three fish ticket

➤ Parent and child, two fish ticket

➤ Evening ticket, two fish (available from May to September)

Oak Lake, Knitsley Mill

It is a short walk to the lakes from the lodge, but disabled anglers can drive up to the edge of the lakes. Knitsley is managed by Jeff Watson who is always around and willing to give sound advice to everyone. Changes are underway at the moment and a new restaurant, with bar, has been opened. Anglers can now have a bacon roll and a bowl of soup with a full-day ticket. Jeff says there are also plans to develop a nine-hole golf course at Knitsley.

Knitsley Mill is a Troutmasters Water and we have fished there many times. Sometimes the fishery gets iced over during the frosty weather but I caught and released thirteen fish one day when the middle lake was two-thirds covered with ice. The fishery is popular, but rarely crowded, and many local anglers enjoy fishing here regularly.

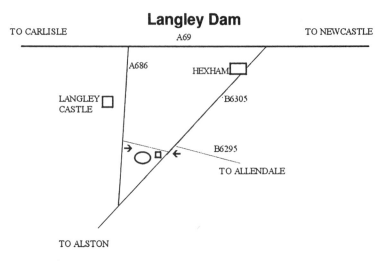

Langley Dam

TO CARLISLE   TO NEWCASTLE

A69

A686

HEXHAM

LANGLEY CASTLE

B6305

B6295

TO ALLENDALE

TO ALSTON

KEY ➜ = FISHERY SIGNPOSTS

Travel tips: Probably the easiest route to Langley Dam is to travel along the A69 from Newcastle to Carlisle and turn off at the A686 junction just before Haydon Bridge. Follow this road, past Langley Castle and a sawmill. Turn left at the Langley, Catton and Allendale junction, (there is a Langley Dam fishery signpost at this turn). Follow this road and the fishery can be seen on your right before the next junction. Turn right at this junction with the A6305 and the entrance is only a few yards on your right. Map not to scale.

Langley Dam Water is a pleasure to fish as it's well stocked and the location is beautiful. Situated eight miles west of Hexham, this fourteen-acre water was originally constructed as a reservoir to supply water for the lead mining industry at Langley. Lead mining has long gone but its legacy is ideal for trout fishing.

The dam wall has fishing spaces separated by bushes but there is ample space for the back cast. One side of the water is lined by a wood and the other side has an extensive reed bed. Wading is possible in the reeded area as the water is shallow but there is a ledge with a drop-off. There are two boats, each of which can be hired by the hour and there are plans to build a jetty for the boats.

The water does contain some brown trout, but good quality rainbows are restocked on a weekly basis. The fishery is open from the first Saturday in March and closes early in November. Anglers can fish seven days a week during the season, from 8am until 9pm or dusk. Langley can take up to thirty rods at any one time.

The lodge is next to the car park and offers tea and coffee facilities.

Rods can be hired and a selection of lures can be bought. There is a microwave if anglers wish to use it and a settee to rest the weary legs.

The fishery offers anglers flexible hours which is useful because people can not always meet set session times of other fisheries. Langley Dam is a Troutmasters fishery and the charges (catch and release) are:

- ➤ 4 hour, three fish ticket
- ➤ 8 hours, five fish ticket
- ➤ Parent and child, 8 hours, six fish ticket

These tickets require that anglers must kill their first three, five or six fish depending upon their ticket, then catch and release.

Another interesting ticket is offered to senior citizens who can fish on Mondays to Thursdays for 8 hours, keep their first three fish then catch and release.

The Langley Dam fishery is managed by Margaret Hope who is always helpful and cheerfully admits to advising anglers how or what flies to use to have a successful day and a visit to Langley Dam is thoroughly recommended.

Playing a fish at Langley Dam

Linnel Wood Lakes

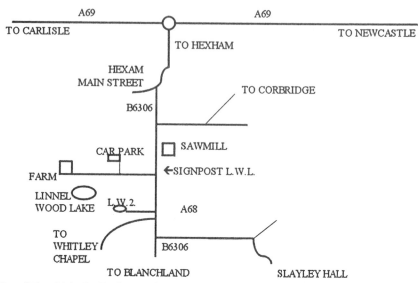

Travel tips: Make for Hexham and its main street. Take the B6306 sign posted off the main street. The lake is about three miles south of Hexham just off this road. Look out for the saw-mill but also a narrow bridge shortly after it. The lake is sign posted l.w.l off the B6306. There is a short walk from the car park to the lake, which is set back and enclosed by woodland. Map not to scale.

Surrounded by mature woodland, the first lake was built by the famous local Charlton family for bird watching. This original, and beautiful, four-and-a-half-acre lake is situated three miles south of the market town of Hexham. It used to be fly only, but a change of management policy has resulted in the lake now being available for both fly and worm fishing. There are casting platforms dotted around the lake. This lake can now take up to a maximum of twenty-five rods. This original lake has two boats, which can be hired by fly fishermen only.

Linnel Wood Lakes are open all year round, but sometimes freeze over during exceptionally cold weather. Anglers are advised to telephone early in the morning should conditions be in any doubt.

There is a walk from the car park to the lake, but the venue is so sheltered and peaceful that the short walk is well worth it. Fishing begins at 8.30am every day and lasts until 9.30pm or dusk.

Fish are restocked regularly, and vary from 1½lbs up to 14lbs.

Even though there are large numbers of rainbow trout the lakes are "topped up" every other day. Tickets available are: a full-day, six fish ticket; half-day, four fish ticket; an evening four fish ticket and a sporting ticket which allows anglers to catch up to ten fish.

Linnel Wood Two Lake is only a short drive from the original lake. This second lake is slightly smaller and is between two and a half and three acres in size. Linnel Wood Two Lake is a fly-only water. This new lake opened in November 1999 and bookings for both lakes are taken on the same telephone number. Advance bookings for either lake are strongly recommended. Cliff Wade is the friendly manager of both lakes and he offers sound advice to all anglers.

Linnel Wood Two Lake takes a maximum of ten fly fishing rods hence the advice to book in advance. This second lake has thirteen casting platforms for the fly fisher. The lake contains mainly rainbows but there are also some brown trout. The trout in this lake vary from one and three-quarter pounds up to double-figure fish. Tickets for the second lake are different from the first lake, and prices are available on request.

Linnel Wood Two Lake is particularly good for buzzer and dry fly fishing. For a peaceful, picturesque venue with good trout these two lakes are well worth a visit.

Linnel Wood, Lake 1

Sharpley Waters

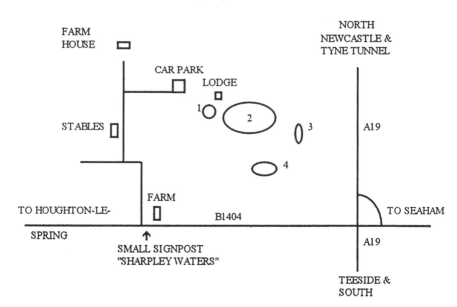

Travel tips: From north or south travel on the A19. Leave A19 at the Seaham turn off (B1404). Travel west approximately 1 mile until you reach the farm buildings on your right and a small signpost (about 1 metre high, marked "Sharpley Waters") on your left. Turn right and follow this small road taking the first right again. Follow the signs until you reach the car park. Map not to scale. 1. Upper Lake. 2. Lower Lake. 3. Dene Lake. 4. New Lake.

Opened in 1997, Sharpley Waters has gained a reputation for providing a good head of hard fighting trout. There are five man-made lakes which are fed with limestone-rich spring water. During 1990, the earth under what is now the largest lake, subsided half a metre due to coal mining activities. This caused drainage problems for crop production, so a series of lakes has been created using the natural clay deposits on the farm.

The largest lake, which covers about three acres, reaches depths of five metres. The water is crystal clear and trout rise at the slightest opportunity. Fish are restocked on a weekly basis from one and a half pounds up to almost twenty pounds. This fishery is open all the year round and never freezes because of its fairly close proximity to the sea. No wading is allowed as casting platforms are provided. Sharpley Waters is also a Troutmaster Water.

The upper and lower lakes at Sharpley Waters

The Strawberry Lake is on the opposite side of the B1404 road and is ideal for disabled angles as cars can be driven right to the lakeside.

Sharpley Waters can accommodate up to forty-two rods and groups are welcomed. There are also special rates for disabled anglers and for parent and child tickets. Tickets and their prices are:

➤ Full-day three fish ticket, then catch and release
➤ Long half-day,(noon until dusk), two fish ticket, then catch and release
➤ Any four hours, one fish then catch and release ticket

On all these tickets you must kill your first fish, then catch and release after your bag limit is reached.

Sporting tickets are:

➤ Full-day
➤ Long half-day, (noon until dusk)
➤ Any four hours

Parent and Child tickets are currently £3 extra on a full-day ticket and £2 extra on a four-hour ticket. Each adult is allowed one child aged between eight and fourteen years.

A happy Paul Hogg, seeing "doubles" at
Sharpley Water *(Sharpley Water)*

The fisherman's lodge at Sharpley Waters is close to the car-park and main lake. The lodge is equipped with a flush toilet, wood stove, electric kettle and microwave oven.

Jack looks after the fishery with Joe (his spaniel). Joe eats anything he is given and sometimes things he is not given – any food that is put down anywhere soon disappears. Jack is a source of honest information about what methods or flies are successful at the time; he even makes and sells a selection of flies from the lodge.

In the future, the owner intends to develop his policy of environmental improvement. Tree planting will continue and a further five new lakes will be opened in the 2001 season. The largest new lake will be 35% bigger than the present largest lake and will have an island in the middle. This lake will take up to thirty rods and will reach depths of twenty feet. Another idea is to devote one of the new lakes to encouraging youngsters and special needs children into the sport. One of the new lakes will be a specimen lake, which will be mainly run on a catch and release system. A golf course is under construction and may be playable by 2003. Sharpley Waters has come a long way in its short lifetime and future plans mean there is a lot more ahead.

Sleekburn Water

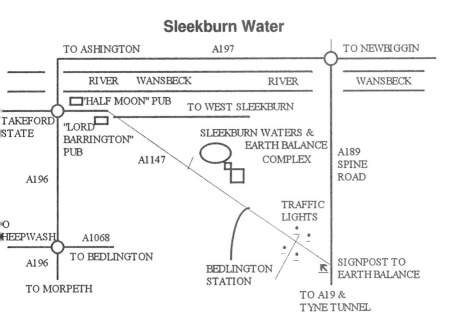

Travel tips: The easiest approach from the south and Newcastle area is to make your way onto the A189 (Spine road). After crossing the River Blyth, take the first left and keep in the left-hand lane until the traffic lights. Keep on the same road, under the railway-bridge and continue for another half a mile where the earth balance complex is on the right. The visitors' entrance is the second turn on the right immediately before the traffic speed camera! You have been warned! From the north the journey is a little more complicated. Anglers need to approach from Morpeth or Ashington. Follow the map to the Half Moon pub at the Stakeford roundabout, then follow the A1147 around the Barrington pub corner and stay on this road. The entrance to the Earth Balance complex is on your left immediately opposite the traffic speed camera, (another warning!). Map not to scale.

Sleekburn Water is a two-and-three-quarter acre fishery that has not been open long. It is building up a good reputation for providing hard-fighting triploid trout from two to twenty pounds. The water is crystal clear and depending on the weather fish can be caught at all levels.

The lake has twelve casting platforms and there is still plenty room to fish from the bank or from the boat that is available. The main platform is immediately in front of the lodge and has been especially designed for disabled anglers. It is good to see wheelchair anglers making regular use of this facility.

Bank fishing takes a maximum of fifteen rods (one of which will be for disabled anglers), with an extra two adult rods in the boat which

Sleekburn Water *(courtesy of Sleekburn Water)*

must be fished from the central buoy. The water is twenty feet at its deepest point. Fish are restocked on a weekly basis.

Sleekburn Waters is only part of the 260-acre site of Earth Balance where natural substances are sustained. The site has its own Terra Firma Café and Organic Bakery which provide food and drink whenever anglers need a break. There is also a visitor centre, brewery, eco trek, organic farming and many other organised activities throughout the year. The car park, which caters for a substantial number of cars, is by the lakeside.

Immaculate toilet facilities are available (together with a specialist disabled one) close to the fishing lodge.

Tickets available at Sleekburn Water are:

➤ Very Early Morning Session, (3am-7am), keep first two fish then catch and release

➤ Full-day ticket, (7am-4pm), keep first two fish then catch and release. This ticket is also available for Parent and Child

➤ Evening Session, (4pm-midnight), keep first two fish then catch and release

➤ Short Sessions, four hours only, from 8am-noon, noon-4pm, and 4pm-8pm. These tickets are a one fish ticket then anglers can catch and release.

In the summer months, for the anglers who cannot sleep or like to get up with the lark, there is the Morning Rise Session. This is a four-hour session that starts at 3am. Anglers can keep two fish, then catch and release. This is reputed to be an excellent time to fish at Sleekburn Water but we have never been able to make that starting time. For those anglers who cannot stay away, there is a generator and halogen lamps available to help anyone fish through the night and arrangements can be made at the lodge. This facility also helps to cater for the many anglers in the area who work shifts. The lake is illuminated with six sets of lights.

Regulars fishing at Sleekburn Waters have also started a membership scheme, which is restricted to 25 anglers. Members can win a prize each month by fishing twice during the month. These anglers can fish at any time that is convenient to them, but they must nominate which particular sessions they wish to be counted for the monthly competition before starting to fish. The monthly winner is the member with the heaviest total bag for their two nominated sessions. At the end of the year, the twelve monthly winners fish for the annual champions trophy.

In connection with Sleekburn Water, Mr Bob Miekle runs a fly tying class on the adjoining Earth Balance complex. The class is held on alternate Wednesdays starting at 7.30pm. During every class, the flies for the following session are decided upon. This enables members to acquire the appropriate hooks and materials. The flies that are tied can always be used at that time of year. It usually finishes when the fishing gossip concludes, somewhere between 9.30 and 10.00pm. It's a friendly class that attracts a growing number of enthusiasts who travel from Newcastle in the south to as far north as Warkworth.

Another advantage at Sleekburn Water is the 24-hour security which is maintained throughout the year. Considering the amount of time that Sleekburn Water has been open, it has established itself as a well-developed small stillwater which contains a healthy stock of hard-fighting trout. It is run by Marty and Mark, two very helpful and hospitable managers. They plan to rear their own fish on site so that they can have a daily stocking system. This means that whatever fish are taken on any day, the same number and weight of fish will be replaced for the following day. *We strongly advise all anglers to make an advance booking for Sleekburn Water.* We have been asked to stress that the needless practice of leaving waste nylon around the fishery has resulted in the death of wild birds, and anyone caught doing this will be asked to leave the area immediately.

Sweethope Loughs

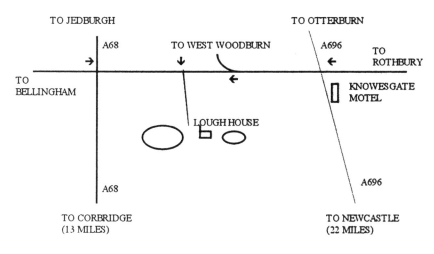

KEY. → = FISHERY SIGNPOSTS.

Travel tips: Travelling on either the A68 or the A696 the loughs are well signposted. The turn off on the A696 is at the Knowesgate Motel. Each required turning after leaving the "A" class roads has signposts and this makes it easy. Map not to scale.

One of the two most northerly fisheries in this book, Sweethope Loughs has a truly tranquil setting in one of the quietest areas in Northumberland.

This fishery is reputed to be one of the oldest in England. Sweethope Loughs consists of two lakes, the Great Lough is 125 acres and the smaller Lough is 24 acres. The Great Lough has a fleet of 20 boats, but also accommodates bank fishing along the south and east banks. No fishing is permitted in the bay where the boats are moored. The smaller Lough used to have two boats on it but these have been removed, so bank fishing is allowed around almost the entire lake.

For safety reasons, no more than two anglers are allowed per boat. The boats are equipped with oars but fishermen can use their own electric motors if they wish. No trolling is permitted from the boats. Wading is allowed on both Loughs, but only thigh waders are suggested on the permit. Most people seem to wear "chesties" but do check when making your booking.

Fishing takes place seven days per week from March 1st to December 31st. Both Loughs are stocked with brown and rainbow trout, the majority being rainbows. Sweethope Loughs are fly only and must be fished with barbless hooks.

Summer sessions are from 9am until 1pm, 1pm until 5pm and 5pm until dusk. Once the dark nights begin to creep in, there are only two sessions, 9am until 1pm and 1pm until dusk. Each four-hour session allows anglers to keep any three fish they catch. Fishing permits are bought from the window at Lough House that stands in the car park. Sweethope is one of the few fisheries that sell National River Authority licences, and it is also a Troutmasters Water.

Sweethope has a beautiful tree-lined setting and offers anglers the chance to catch trout up to 20lbs plus from both bank and boat. Sporting tickets and Season tickets are available on request.

Sweethope expects to stock over 26,000 triploid rainbows averaging 2¾lbs. Also, 2,000 home-reared brown trout weighing up to 1½lbs will also be introduced to the two Loughs during a season. Sweethope remains a popular venue where many anglers choose to return time after time. After fishing these Loughs it is easy to understand Sweethope's attraction.

The small lough

Witton Castle Lakes

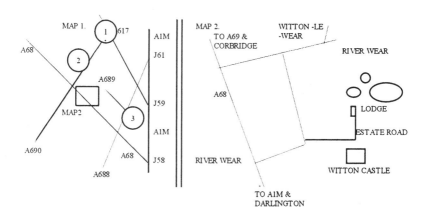

Travel tips: The easiest route to Witton Castle Lakes is to journey onto the A68 from either the north or the south. From the north travel along the A68 and cross the River Wear which is signposted. Just over the bridge, and as the road begins to bend, take the first left. Travelling from the south, this road is obviously on the right, just before the River Wear bridge. On leaving the A68, this secondary road goes down the hill towards a narrow bridge. Immediately before this small bridge the entrance to Witton Castle Estate and Lakes is on your right between two tall stone gateposts. Follow the estate road/track on to the fishery car park. Map not to scale. Key: 1. Durham. 2. Crook. 3. Bishop Auckland.

Set in open meadowland of the Wear valley, Witton Castle Lakes fishery is found in the grounds of the Witton Castle Estate. This fishery is the stillwater section of the Bishop Auckland Angling Club.

It is situated near to the A68 in the south of County Durham and has three lakes. South Holme Lake is three acres in size, West Holme is four acres and East Holme is the largest at fourteen acres. All three lakes lie close to each other. Each contains both brown and rainbow trout, but all browns, if caught, must be returned. The rainbows are restocked on a weekly basis, and vary between 2 and 12lbs in weight.

Witton Castle Lakes is a Troutmasters water and their season begins on the weekend closest to 27th February and lasts until the week-end nearest to 28th November. Daily fishing begins at 8am and ends at dusk.

All fishing in these clear-water gravel pits is from the bank with no wading allowed. Every angler is required to carry their own priest and landing net. Each angler can catch a maximum of eight fish per day. On a sporting ticket, all fish must be returned, but there is no maxi-

Jack McGuire plays a fish at Witton Castle

mum number of fish can be caught on this ticket. On a full-day ticket, the first fish must be killed and, thereafter, the angler can choose to keep any two fish from the next seven. Further tickets can be bought if anyone wishes to fish on after catching their eight fish limit. A Parent and Child (under 16), ticket is also available and means the two combined rods can keep their first four fish and return a maximum of five fish each.

Bill and Ken are the two syndicate members who regularly man the lodge where tickets and a small selection of tackle is available. These two lads are friendly, and always worth listening to for successful tactics.

Witton Castle Lakes has a good sized car-park with spaces closest to the lodge reserved for disabled anglers. The lodge is brick built and incorporates the toilet facilities. Meals can be bought from the Castle or nearby public houses. It is only a very short walk from the lodge to the lakes which makes fishing comparatively easy for disabled anglers.

Private Fisheries at a Glance

	Beamish	Hadrian	Jubilee	Knitsley	Langley	Linnel	Starpley	Sleekburn	Sweethope	Witton
Size (acres)	1.5	0.6	3	5.5	14	9	6	3	150	21
Tuition	Y		Y	Y	Y	Y	Y	Y	Y	Y
Toilet	Y	Y	Y	Y	Y		Y	Y	Y	Y
Tackle Shop (for sale)	Y		Y	Y					Y	Y
(for hire)	Y									
Flies (for sale)	Y		Y		Y		Y		Y	Y
Boats			Y	Y	Y			Y	Y	
Disabled	Y		Y	Y	Y		Y	Y	Y	
Wading (allowed)	Y				Y				Y	
Landing Nets Provided			Y							
Refreshment: Hot Drinks		Y	Y	Y	Y		Y	Y		
Cold Drinks		Y	Y					Y	Y	
Hot Food		Y	Y					Y		
Snacks / Sandwiches		Y	Y					Y	Y	
Lodge	Y	Y	Y	Y	Y	Y	Y	Y		Y
Car Park to Water (short)	Y	Y	Y	Y	Y		Y	Y	Y	Y
(long)					Y					
Fish Storage Facilities	Y		Y							
Troutmasters Water	Y		Y	Y	Y		Y		Y	Y
Barbless Hooks	Y	Y	Y	Y	Y	Y	Y	Y	Y	Y
Catch and Release	Y	Y	Y	Y	Y	Y	Y	Y	Y	Y
Fly	Y	Y	Y	Y	Y	Y	Y	Y	Y	Y
Worm	Y				Y					
Sporting Ticket	Y						Y	Y		Y
Casting Platforms	Y			Y		Y	Y	Y	Y	

Alan Young with a Fontburn Double

Northumbrian Water Fisheries

Northumbrian Water fisheries attract around 55,000 anglers per year. In a region which stretches from the Cheviot Hills to the Pennine Dales and the North York Moors, the company manages 22 sites. Most of the reservoirs contain Brown and Rainbow trout, while Fontburn is the only water to stock Brook trout too.

The policy of Northumbrian Water is to welcome the public and to provide great opportunities to follow a wide range of leisure pursuits, especially trout fishing. All the fisheries can be divided into two sections, premier and leased fisheries. Fishing on certain waters is leased to angling clubs, most of whom offer a small number of day tickets, and details can be found when telephoning the contact numbers quoted later in this section.

Premier fisheries are managed by Northumbrian Water and wardens have been appointed to oversee the running of these reservoirs. All the Premier waters have many things in common, exceptions being mentioned under the individual reservoir headings. Nearly all Premier Fisheries allow worm and fly fishing at some stage of the season. These fisheries open at 6am and close one hour after sunset. They have a bag limit of eight fish on a full-day ticket. Day permits – £14 or £12 (concessionary) – can be obtained from machines that take £2, £1 and 50p coins. To encourage junior anglers (under-17), the company allows two youngsters to fish free on an adult ticket sharing the bag limit. Two season tickets are available:

➤ **Gold Explorer:** which allows anglers to keep up to 42 fish per week and a maximum of 8 fish per day. Cost in 2001: £599

➤ **Silver Explorer:** which allows anglers to keep up to 24 fish per week and 8 fish per day. Cost in 2001: £509

These tickets allow fishing on any of Northumbrian Water Premier Waters on every day of the season. Anglers must, however, leave the water once they have caught their bag limit (eight fish at most reservoirs, and twelve at Cow Green). Although Explorer tickets might seem expensive, they may be a sound investment compared to buying one-day tickets. To purchase these, contact: Northumbrian Water Recreation Department, Abbey Road, Pity Me, Durham DH1 5FJ. Telephone: 0191 383 2222.

Environmental Agency Rod Licences are available at Fontburn and Kielder reservoirs. Note: Whittle Dene is a syndicated trout fishery, for members only. Public trout fishing ceased at the end of the 2000 season and the waters have been converted for *coarse fishing*.

Northumbrian Water Premier Fisheries

Northern Area
   Fontburn: 01669 621 368
   Kielder: 01434 240 396
   Whittle Dene: 01207 255 250

Central Area
   Derwent: 01207 255 250

South-East Area
   Scaling Dam: 0191 383 2222

South-West Area
   Grassholme: 01833 50204
   Blackton: 01833 650 204
   Hury: 01833 650 204
   Cow Green: 01833 650 204

Northumbrian Water Leased Fisheries

Northern Area
   Catcleugh: 0191 386 3803
   Colt Crag: 01434 606 862
   Little Swinburne: 01434 606 862
   East & West Hallington: 01434 681 405

Central Area
   Smiddyshaw: 01207 501 237
   Waskerly: 01207 290 964
   Tunstall: 01388 527 293

South-East Area
   Lockwood Beck: 01287 660 501

South-West Area
   Burnhope: 01913 832 222; ext: 36960

Premier Fisheries are now covered in more detail; anglers wishing to fish the leased waters are advised to telephone for further information. The Premier Fisheries are in no particular order other than being grouped by location.

NORTHERN AREA

Fontburn Reservoir

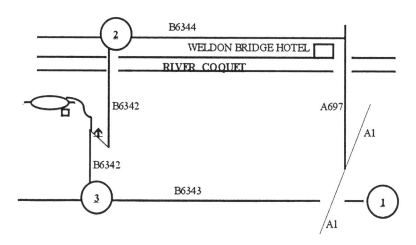

Travel tips: The easiest route to Fontburn Reservoir is to travel on the A697 and turn off at Weldon Bridge onto the Rothbury road (B6344). In Rothbury itself take the first main turn on the left onto the B6342 and after crossing the river, bear left on the main road. Continue on this road (up and down) for approximately 6-7 miles until there is a sharp right bend followed by a sharp left. Just on this sharp left bend is the signpost for the reservoirs. This is the start of the reservoir road. Follow this single-track road past the farm buildings and on to the fishery. When you meet the dam wall "T" junction, turn left and the lodge is about 200 yards around to your right. Map not to scale. Key: 1. Morpeth. 2. Rothbury. 3. Scots Gap

Fontburn Reservoir is found in a small valley of the Simonside Hills about seven miles south of Rothbury. This reservoir is 87 acres and its western end there is a nature reserve where fishing is prohibited.

Anglers can worm or fly fish from anywhere around the fishing area. When the water level is high, fly fishing is stopped on the dam wall (if unsure, ask at the lodge). To help fly fishermen, the fishery implemented a tree felling programme to create more fly fishing areas.

Concern for disabled anglers has resulted in Fontburn having a floating jetty that has easy access. The jetty has railed supporting sides which makes it safe for wheelchair anglers. The car-park on the north side of the reservoir is almost at the start of the jetty.

The lodge has a coin machine for permits, a table with bench seats, a hot drinks machine, scales and a machine for worms, floats and basic tackle. Immediately behind this room are the toilets (including disabled). The senior wardens can be contacted on 01669 621 368.

Fontburn attracts many anglers because of its reputation for big fish. Latest figures show the record rainbow is *twenty-six and a half pounds*, the record brown trout is nine and a quarter pounds and the record brook trout, (which is a national record), is eight pounds three ounces. Fontburn has produced twenty-two trout weighing over ten pounds in one week

Most of the heavy fish are caught on worm although fly fishing does account for a reasonable number of big fish. No other Northumbrian Water fishery can boast the numbers and weight of these large fish, which are landed regularly at Fontburn. The latest figures show that Fontburn attracts over 10,000 angler visits per season and they catch nearly 22,000 trout.

Fontburn Reservoir

Kielder Reservoir

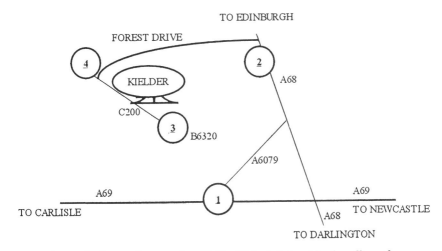

Travel tips: The favoured approach to Kielder Water is to head for the village of Bellingham. Head west through the village, and just as the road bends to cross the river North Tyne, the C200 road leaves on your right. Kielder Water is well signposted at this junction. Follow this road and it takes you to Kielder Water and the Visitors Centre at Tower Knowe. The view as you come over the top of the hill above Kielder Water is breathtaking. Map not to scale. Key: 1. Hexham. 2. Jedburgh. 3. Bellingham. 4. Kielder

One of the largest lakes in northern Europe, covering 2,700 acres, Kielder Reservoir was created in 1982. With its 27 miles of shoreline, it is the flagship of Northumbrian Water and it is located in the centre of Northumberland National Park at the head of the North Tyne valley. Kielder is surrounded by Britain's largest coniferous forest and is close to the Scottish border.

The Kielder experience definitely brings everyone close to nature because of its wide-ranging environments. There are many leisure activities to experience at Kielder, trout fishing being just one.

During the early days, Kielder had only brown trout but rainbows were stocked to encourage day tickets. Day tickets allow anglers to keep eight fish. Fifty motorised coble boats are available from 8:30am to 5pm but must be returned by 8pm. In October boats are available from 9am to 3.30pm. Boats must have a minimum of two people, a maximum of three and can be booked on (01434) 250312. Kielder season lasts from May 1st until October 31st, and the worm fishing begins on June 1st. This reservoir is very deep and the majority of all trout caught are in the margins (within 35metres of the shore).

Kielder also hosts the English National eliminator fly fishing boat competition. Almost 3,000 anglers are attracted per season and they catch around 7,700 trout. This is one of the few fisheries where fishermen can stay, with 32 cabins available for visiting families. There are also 30 pitches for backpackers, and 118 caravans can be accommodated in twelve acres of woodland. Your stay could be divided between fishing and your family. The whole area can be explored on horseback, foot, cycle or in the cabin cruiser "The Osprey". Water sports include wind surfing, boating and water-skiing.

Very briefly, there are three main centres around the reservoir: Leaplish Waterside Park, Tower Knowe Visitor Centre and Kielder Castle. At Leaplish there is an indoor swimming pool, cycle hire facilities, crazy golf, children's play area, a restaurant and a "Birds of Prey" centre. Tower Knowe has a visitor centre and an exhibition which shows the history and the development of the area over the last five-hundred million years. Kielder Castle has the Forest Visitor Centre, a craft shop, restaurant and a "Birds of Kielder" exhibition. From here, there is also the "Forest Drive" which links Kielder with the A68. During the year there are many special events organised, such as Husky dog sledge racing and cyclo-orienteering events.

Jetty and boats at Kielder Water *(courtesy of Northumbrian Water)*

CENTRAL AREA
Derwent Reservoir

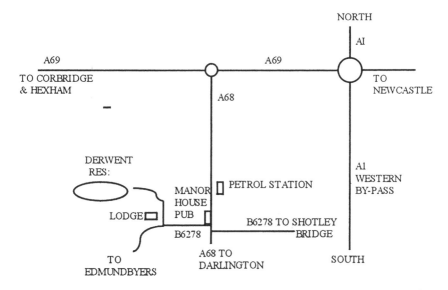

Travel tips: From the south, travel on the A68 and from the North journey on the A69 until you meet the A68. From either direction ignore any Derwent Reservoir signposts until the junction with the B6278, (this is easy to spot with petrol station on one side of the road and the "Manor House" pub opposite). Travel down the hill at this junction immediately before a small stone bridge, turn right, the lodge is in front of you on the left. Car parking is immediately beyond the lodge. After payment at the lodge, drive up the hill to the reservoir.
Map not to scale

Opened in 1966, Derwent Reservoir is three and a half miles long and one mile wide. For the trout fishermen this reservoir provides seven miles of bank fishing among the hills between Weardale and Northumberland. Anglers can fly fish from anywhere except the west end nature reserve and the sailing club area. Worm fishermen are restricted to the south bank (but this is three miles long). This means there is always ample space even on busy days. Anglers do not need to pre book at Derwent Reservoir, and permits can be bought next to the warden's office or at the Post Office at nearby Edmundbyers.

The road across the dam wall, which connects the warden's office to the south bank, is a one-way system. So, once across, to fill in your catch return, you must continue to meet the B6278 road that skirts the

Derwent Reservoir

southern shore and return to the entrance of the reservoir. There are three picnic sites around the lake. Toilet facilities vary, and one fisherman described them as "Not brilliant but adequate".

Northumbrian Water organises different events at Derwent throughout the year. "Come Fishing" courses, usually about May or July, provide tuition for the complete beginner to the more experienced who wish to improve their casting techniques.

Both worm and fly fishing methods are taught to all anglers, from the youngest, about eight, to senior citizens, but the youngest age for fly fishing tuition is twelve years. There are three-hour sessions for beginners with everything (tackle and licences) provided. These courses are very popular and, as places are limited, early booking is recommended.

Derwent also hosts a number of competitions. There are the eliminators for the House of Hardy competition. Another big competition, probably the biggest worm trout fishing competition in England, is the "Giant Wriggler".

As Derwent is so popular, the reservoir season is usually extended until the end of November. Stocking is continued, but fishing is

Alan Young fishing the north bank

restricted from 8am until 4pm. Permit prices are reduced, and bag limits are increased to twelve fish per angler.

This a very scenic reservoir and has a long low shoreline, with very few trees near the water, which makes it easier for anyone who wishes to fly fish. Talking to a regular angler, who started casting a line there about eighteen months after the reservoir opened, it appears that Derwent once had boats for hire. A fleet of about eight or nine boats could be hired but this facility is no longer available.

Another successful season at Derwent has been reported and the latest figures show the reservoir had 12,410 anglers fishing and they caught a total of 29,883 trout. This is an incredible number of anglers and it speaks volumes for the work done by the staff at the reservoir.

Northumbrian Water has introduced a catch and return system for fly fishing anglers. This means that fly fishermen can catch and release as many trout as they wish, but once they have killed eight fish they must leave the water.

The idea of introducing the catch and release ticket is to encourage conservation, which youngsters are taught about at school, and hopefully to increase the number of female anglers. Many anglers do not necessarily wish to kill their fish.

Another new ticket, which will be available at Derwent and at Scaling Dam, is called the "Stress Buster". This ticket will allow anglers to fish from 3pm, and to wind down after work. The latest figures show that the Derwent reservoir is the most popular Northumbrian Water fishery. This reservoir attracts almost 12,500 angler visits resulting in 29,883 trout being caught.

SOUTH-WEST AREA

Lying reasonably close to each other, in south-west Durham, and on quite high land, are the reservoirs of Grassholme, Blackton, Hury and Cow Green.

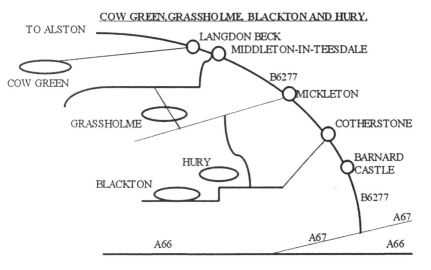

Travel tips: From Hexham, head to Alston and follow the B6277 road. Then follow signposts for each village and the reservoir. Map not to scale.

Grassholme

Grassholme Reservoir is set in Lunedale and is surrounded by meadowland. It is one and a half miles west of Mickleton, off the B6277, and is 140 acres in size. This is a popular reservoir to fish with both fly and worm. Disabled facilities are provided at toilets, parking areas and there is a sizeable concrete shoreline to fish from.

A visitor centre opened in 1993 with an information display room, fishing lodge, wardens office and toilets. There is also a tearoom which opens during bank holidays and weekends. This facility provides a selection of hot and cold food.

Grassholme also plays host to the Teesdale Angling weekend. During one weekend there are fly and worm competitions on Saturday and Sunday. One day is the adult competition and the following day is the junior competition (under-17). The junior competition, which is now held at the Derwent reservoir, has two sections, under

13, and 13-17s. There is also a special prize for the best girl entrant. The latest figures show that 7,700 angler visits produced 16,766 trout.

Blackton

Blackton is one mile west of Hury reservoir and is 66 acres in size. There is only fly fishing allowed on this beautiful small water. Permits can be bought at the coin machine on site or at Cotherstone Post Office. The latest figures show that 3,430 angler visits produced 7,811 trout.

Hury

This reservoir has a beautiful setting on the River Balder and is popular with anglers. Hury lies west of Romaldkirk, off the B6277 and is 120 acres. Anglers can bank fish and use either fly or worming methods. The latest figures show that 7,256 angler visits produced 16,226 trout.

Cow Green

Cow Green Reservoir is the highest of the Northumbrian Water fisheries. The water is surrounded by Pennine moorland and covers 770 acres.

This fishery differs from its sister reservoirs in that it contains only brown trout. It is reputed to have one of the best populations of brown trout in England. The daily bag limit is twelve fish, and anglers can use either fly or worm. Fishing is prohibited along the south-east shore from the lodge, up to, and including, the dam wall. There is no ticket machine at this water, and payment is made by a self-service envelope system. The cost for fishing Cow Green is also cheaper than other Northumbrian Water reservoirs. The latest figures show that 354 angler visits produced 664 trout.

SOUTH-EAST AREA

Scaling Dam

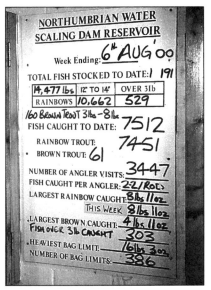

NORTHUMBRIAN WATER
SCALING DAM RESERVOIR

Week Ending: 6ᵗʰ AUG '00

TOTAL FISH STOCKED TO DATE: 1 191

| 14,477 lbs | 12" TO 14" | OVER 3lb |
| RAINBOWS | 10,662 | 529 |

160 BROWN TROUT 3lbs -8lbs
FISH CAUGHT TO DATE: 7512

RAINBOW TROUT: 7451
BROWN TROUT: 61

NUMBER OF ANGLER VISITS: 3447
FISH CAUGHT PER ANGLER: 2·2/Rods
LARGEST RAINBOW CAUGHT: 8lbs 11oz
THIS WEEK 8lbs 11oz
LARGEST BROWN CAUGHT: 4lbs 11oz
FISH OVER 3lb CAUGHT 303
HEAVIEST BAG LIMIT: 16lbs 3oz
NUMBER OF BAG LIMITS: 386

Information board for Scaling Dam

Scaling Dam is a popular fishery for anglers in the south-east of the region. Its 105 acres are surrounded by wild moorland. This water lies adjacent to the A171, between Guisborough and Whitby.

Fishing is from the bank and anglers can choose to worm or fly fish. There are facilities for disabled anglers at the toilets, fishing lodge, car-park and at the jetty. Disabled anglers must note that their permits are only available at the disabled lodge where there is an envelope system and not a machine (RADAR key is needed). The latest figures show that 5,283 angler visits caught 11,253 trout.

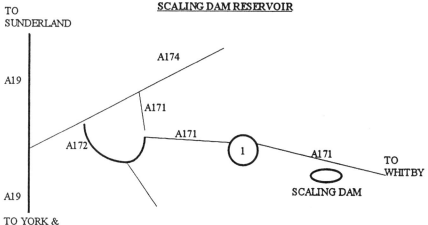

Travel tips: Easiest route is to get onto the A19 and follow the signs for Whitby via the A174 and the A171. Follow the A171 through Guisborough and Scaling Dam lies immediately south of this road. The entrance for the fishing lodge is before reaching "The Grapes" public house as you travel east. Map not to scale.

Disabled platform overlooking Scaling Dam reservoir

Northumbrian Water Fisheries at a glance

	Stock	Season	Times	Methods	Bag limit	Prices
Fontburn Reservoir	B-W R-S Br-S	22/3-30/9	7am to time on site	bank: F & Wo	8	£14 – Fu £12 – C
Derwent Reservoir	B-W&S R-S	B: 1/5-31/10 R: 22/3-31/10 F: 22/3	6am to time on site	south bank: F&Wo dam & north bank: fly	8	£14 – Fu £12 – C
Kielder	B-W R-S	B: 1/5-31/10 R: same fly: May worm: June	6am to 9pm or 1pm to sunset*	bank: F&Wo boat: F&Wo	8	£12 – Fu £10 – C boats: £22 we £15 mw
Grass-holme	B-W R-S	B: 1/5-3/10 R: same fly:May worm: June	6am to 9pm or 1pm to sunset*	bank	8	£14 – Fu £12 – C
Blackton	B-W&S R-S	B: 1/5-3/10 R: same fly: May worm: June	6am to 9pm or 1pm to sunset*	bank: F only	8	£16 – Fu £13 – C
Hury	B-W&S R-S	22/10-30/9 22/3-31/10	6am to 9pm or 1pm to sunset*	bank: F only	8	£14 – Fu £12 – C
Cow Green	B-W	22/3-30/9	6 am to 1 hour after sunset	bank: F & Wo	12	£7 – Fu £6 – C
Scaling Dam	B-W R-S	22/3-30/9 22/3-31/10	6am to 1 hour after sunset	bank: F & Wo	8	£14 – Fu £12 – C

Key:
B – brown; R – rainbow; S – stock; F – fly; W – wild; Wo – worm; * – whichever is earlier; we – weekend; mw – mid-week; Br – brook; Fu – full; C – concessionary

Hanningfield Trout Fishery

Anyone travelling south due to work commitments or on holiday, should note that a current Explorer ticket entitles you to fish at Hanningfield Trout Fishery, which is managed by Essex and Suffolk Water (a sister company of Northumbrian Water). Hanningfield is stocked with rainbow and brown trout, and their season is from 28th March to 31st October. It is a 'fly fishing only' water and opens daily from 8am until one hour after dusk. Unlike the waters in Northumbria, the bag limit at Hanningfield is six fish.

Hanningfield caters predominately for boat anglers and has a reputation for large, grown-on fish of excellent quality and they are hard fighters. The fishing lodge has a well-stocked tackle shop and a cafeteria which provides light refreshments. Tuition is available, although a prior booking must be made for this facility. There is also a smokery with smoked and unsmoked trout available. Frozen and fresh trout can also be bought. Enquires and bookings can be made for Hanningfield at the shop (01268 710 101) or at their office (01245 212 031).

Flies for Northumbrian Waters

The following flies for use on Northumbrian Waters have been suggested by the Senior Wardens responsible for each reservoir:

Fontburn Reservoir

Dawson's Olive. Viva. Montana Nymph. Muddler Minnow. Black and Peacock; pider. Black Pennell. Peter Ross. Baby Doll.

Kielder Reservoir

Any small dark traditional fly. Montana Nymph. Baby Doll. Black and Peacock. Muddler Minnow. Sedge Pupa. Cinnamon and Gold. Dog Nobbler. Pheasant Tail Nymph. Black Midge. Hare's Ear Sedge.

Derwent Reservoir

Fritz (orange, black or white). Daddies. Hoppers. Bibio. Black Buzzer. Pheasant Tail. NymphCats Whisker. Kate Maclaren. Black C.D.C. Dawson's Olive.

Grassholme Reservoir

Black Buzzer. Zulu. Viva. Black Pennell. Teal and Black. Peter Ross. Muddler Minnow.

Blackton

Daddies. Sedges. Dawson's Olive. Zulu. Viva. Peter Ross. Black Pennell. Teal and Black. Kate Maclaren.

Hury

Zulu. Black Pennell. Peter Ross. Viva. Bibio. Muddler Minnow. Teal and Black.

Cow Green Reservoir

Kate Maclaren. Bibio. Zulu. Black and Peacock Spider. Invicta. Ke-He. Black Pennell. Mallard and Claret. Gold Ribbed Hare's Ear. Butcher. Dunkeld. Midge Pupa. Wickham's Fancy.

Scaling Dam Reservoir

Montana Nymph. Viva. Dawson's Olive. Hawthorn Fly. Invicta. Wickham's Fancy. Kate Maclaren. Hoppers. Baby Doll. Appetiser.

Methods of Fishing

There are many good and varied books on the shelves that deal with
how to fish and we do not propose to go into methods in any great
detail, but we feel it is important to lay a background introduction to
the different styles and so this section is a very brief insight into these
styles.

Lure Fishing

Lures tend to be the larger, more vividly coloured flies. All stillwaters
have their own rules on fly sizes, or the number of hook points
allowed (which may cut out the use of double and treble hooks).
Some waters allow only a single-hook fly, so it is advisable to check if
fishing a "new" water. Many lures do not represent any food form and
the movement, which in turn stimulates aggression, attracts the
trout. Other lures have been designed to represent the larger food
forms and can be fished at all depths but tend to concentrate on mid
to deeper water. Lures can be fished at different speeds, but if an
angler detects a take then sometimes this can be converted into a fish
by speeding up the retrieve.

Anglers must be prepared to try different retrieves and depths to
find the fish. Lure fishing can be very productive and is the favourite
method of fishing for many anglers.

Nymph Fishing

Nymphs can and will be found in all depths of the water. From the
lakebed, where they leave their larval cases, they swim freely to the
surface to hatch and the trout are waiting to feed on them at all stages.
Some nymphs will stay on the lake bottom for some time before they
fully develop but, for others, it is a relatively short period before they
must make the perilous journey to adulthood. Nymphs form a major
part of the trout's diet and a spooned fish can be found to be full of
them.

Nymphs are probably fished best on a floating line with a long
leader as this method tends to keep the fly from snagging in the weed
on the lake bed. A sinking line can, of course, be used if desired but
we have found this only adds to the snagging problem.

An unweighted fly can be used to explore the surface of the water and just below, while a lightly weighted fly will sink that little bit deeper. A heavily weighted fly will cover lower depths, otherwise an intermediate line may be the answer to finding the correct depth. Be prepared to experiment with size, colour and speed of retrieve as some nymphs can move with astonishing speed when they need to.

Damsel Nymph, Montana Nymph, Gold Ribbed Hares Ear and Pheasant Tail Nymphs are all popular dressings and are well worth having in the fly box.

Fishing The Wet Fly

Wet fly fishing is exactly what it says, namely fishing a fly beneath the surface of the water. Many wet flies are designed to imitate a specific part of the trout's diet such as a hatching sedge or midge. Peter Ross, Mallard and Claret, Butcher, Blae and Black and Invicta are all wet fly patterns that have stood the test of time and continue to catch trout on all waters.

Traditional wet fly fishing from a slowly drifting boat is a very enjoyable form of fishing. As the boat drifts, the angler can cover a large area of water and thus cover more fish. This method involves using a leader with up to three droppers, each with the preferred fly attached. Short casts are made in front of the boat as it drifts down the water and the retrieve is just enough to keep in contact with the flies. Fish can and will take right up to the boat and are willing to take a fly just as it is being lifted off the water.

This method is best in a slight wave or ripple – a flat calm is not the best condition for this style. Wet fly fishing from the bank can be just as productive and anglers must be prepared for some vicious takes.

As we have said before, anglers must be prepared to experiment until they find what fly the fish want and at what depth and speed they are taking them.

Fishing The Dry Fly

Dry flies are flies that are designed to be fished on the surface of the water. Some anglers enjoy this method of fishing most of all because they can "match the hatch" and watch the trout take the fly. "Matching the hatch" simply means watching what flies are hatching on the surface of the water and presenting the trout with a fly that is as close to the natural in size, colour and shape as possible. Once the fly has been cast, the angler then needs to introduce as similar a movement to their fly as the natural, if movement is required at all. Often dry flies need not be moved and the trout will take them "static".

Anglers can also target individual trout as they watch them feeding. The dry fly is cast in the projected path of the cruising trout but presentation and delicate casting is all important and finer terminal tackle is often required. It is also important to remember that trout see floating flies as a silhouette so the size and shape are important factors.

It is not uncommon when anglers are fishing the dry fly to think they have a take and that the fish has missed the fly. This is not necessarily so because trout sometimes try to "drown" the fly by swamping it with water. They then turn and take it at their leisure. It is a failing of some anglers to strike too quickly and this only pulls the fly from the fish's mouth. The angler must give the fish time to take the fly before lifting the rod and an old adage is to say "God save the Queen" before striking. This allows the fish time to take the hook into its mouth and often results in more fish on the bank and less swearing over the water.

As with any method of fly fishing, anglers learn by experimentation, and dry fly fishing can be an exciting and enjoyable technique.

Tying your own flies

To catch your first fly-caught trout is an exciting experience, probably one that will be remembered all your life. To catch a trout with a fly that you have tied yourself gives you a further sense of satisfaction and fulfilment.

Much enjoyment can be gained by tying your own flies, especially when it is impossible to make it to the water and cast a rod. Mastering the very basic skills is easy, and once anglers have tied one or two of the easier patterns, and caught fish with them, then a whole new aspect of trout fishing opens up.

There is a wealth of help to support the novice fly tyer. Locally, some schools run night classes that attract all levels of ability. Local fishing clubs also meet one night per month to help each other to increase members' skills. Bookshops in our area carry a range of fly tying books. There are books to suit all pockets, but a sound investment is Peter Gathercole's "The Handbook of Fly Tying". It contains many good, clear, close-up photographs, suggested materials for all the different stages of fly production and detailed step-by-step information on how to tie the flies.

Another useful source of help is in the monthly trout fishing magazines. This source usually keeps anglers up to date with the very latest successful flies, new materials or variations of flies already in use. These magazines are a worthwhile investment and are a constant source of interest and information.

Good, basic fly tying tools or kits are available from most tackle shops or catalogues. A clean, white work-top and a good light source are advisable to work with.

Becoming a fly tyer also brings its own problems – nothing is safe. The sleeping cat or dog, a tuft of the carpet or coloured rug suddenly becomes a source of interest, and collectable! Nail varnish, clear or coloured is borrowed or bought, although it does make others suspicious of your intentions! But joking apart, fly tying is a relaxing, enjoyable hobby which also adds to the anticipation of your next fishing trip.

The ultimate in fly tying is to design a successful fly and have it named after yourself. One of the best examples from this region was achieved by Brian Dawson. Brian designed the very successful Dawson's Olive, which is now not only nationally, but internationally recognised as a consistent taker of trout.

Our Fly Selection

We now include a selection of our favourite flies and their patterns.
These patterns are what we use, but there are many variations to each
fly and the individual tyer can adapt them to suit their own require-
ments. Throughout, l/s = long shank.

Lures

Appetiser

Hook	l/s 8 - 12
Silk	black
Tail	mixed dark green and orange fibres with silver mallard breast feathers
Body	white chenille
Rib	fine oval silver tinsel
Beard	as for tail
Wing	white marabou
Over-wing	grey squirrel tail fibres

A very effective fly pattern. This fly, invented by Bob Church, will take
fish at all waters but we have found it most effective at the beginning and
more towards the end of the season when trout are feeding up on fry for
the winter.

Ace of Spades

Hook	l/s 6 - 10
Silk	black
Body	black chenille
Rib	oval silver tinsel
Wing	two black feathers tied "matuka" style
Over-wing	dark bronze mallard
Beard	guinea fowl fibres

A very killing pattern indeed, especially at the beginning of the season.
Created by Dave Collyer of Surrey, a "Matuka" style fly but with an
over-wing or veil of bronze mallard.

Baby doll

Hook	l/s 6 - 10
Silk	black
Body	white nylon baby wool
Back	as body
Tail	as body
Head	built up with tying silk

A simple small fry imitation that has accounted for many fish. This fly is also very effective when tied in peach or fluorescent lime green.

Cat's Whisker

Hook	l/s 6 - 12
Silk	black
Eyes	chain bead
Tail	white marabou
Rib	oval silver tinsel
Body	fluorescent yellow, or-ange, or green chenille
Wing	white marabou

Cat's Whisker

This lure will take fish all year round and may be fished at all depths. The original colours are white and green but other colours work well and a few strands of holographic tinsel seem to give added attraction.

Fritz

Hook	l/s 8 - 10
Silk	black
Eyes	brass bead chain
Tail	marabou with a few strands of pearl lureflash
Body	fritz
Wing	as for tail

Another modern lure made with new materials. We have found all colours work well throughout the year. Experiment with colour and depth until you find the fish.

Dawson's Olive

Hook	l/s 8 - 10
Silk	orange
Tail	orange or yellow marabou
Body	olive chenille
Wing	olive marabou
Beard	blue dyed guinea fowl

We feel this is one of the best lures ever devised. It will take fish all year round at all depths and in all conditions.

Viva

Hook	l/s 6 - 12
Silk	black
Tail	fluorescent green wool
Rib	silver tinsel
Body	black chenille
Wing	4 black cock hackles or black marabou
Beard	black cock hackle fibres

A popular fly on Northern waters but not used as much as it deserves. This fly has been and still is a very killing pattern.

Zonker

Hook	l/s 8 - 10
Silk	black
Body	pearl mylar
Back/Wing	a few strands of flashabou under a strip of rabbit
Hackle	cock hackle fibres

Zonker

An excellent lure in recent years and based on the New Zealand rabbit style lures. Very effective when fished deep or along the bottom of the lake or reservoir. This fly accounts for many double-figure fish.

Nymphs

Pheasant Tail Nymph

Hook	8 - 14
Silk	black or brown
Tail	bunch of cock pheasant tail fibres
Rib	copper or silver wire
Body as	for tail
Thorax	as for tail
thorax cover	as for tail
Legs	as for tail (tips)

Note: thorax can be of silver or pearl lurex

This nymph can be tied hooks ranging from a long-shank 8 to a small size 14 or even 16. Although this fly does not represent any particular nymph, its size and shape cover a wide spectrum of the trout's diet.

Damsel Nymph

Hook	l/s 8 - 10
under body	lead wire (vary amount for different depths)
Silk	olive
Tail	3 dyed olive hackle points
Rib	fine gold wire
Abdomen	dyed olive feather fibres
Thorax	light olive seal's fur
Hackle	brown partridge
wing-cases & head	olive feather fibres

A great fly in summer when the naturals are on the wing, but will take fish throughout the year.

Montana Nymph

Hook	l/s 10 - 12
Silk	black
Tail	black cock fibres
Body	black chenille
Thorax	yellow chenille

Hackle	black cock (over thorax only)
wing case	as body

A proven all-round nymph pattern which will take fish on all waters. Usually a large nymph pattern, but we have found it can be very good when tied in the smaller sizes.

Montana nymph

Gold Ribbed Hare's Ear

hook	any size seems to work well but not too big
silk	brown/ beige
tail	hares body guard hair
rib 1	wide flat gold lurex
rib 2	fine gold wire (over rib 1)
body	hare or rabbit fur
thorax	as body but with guard hair well picked out
wing-cases	cock pheasant tail fibres

Gold Ribbed Hare's Ear

A fly pattern we would never be without. It can be tied with a gold bead head to give it extra depth, but still one of the best nymph patterns available to the angler of today.

Wet Flies

Bibio

hook	8 - 14
silk	black˙
rib	silver wire
body	black-red-black seal's fur
hackle	palmered black cock

Originating in Ireland, but a very popular pattern in this area. We have found it best fished in or just below the surface film.

Peter Ross

hook	10 - 14
silk	black
tail	golden pheasant tippet
rib	fine oval silver wire
body	rear half: silver tinsel; front half: red seal's fur
hackle	soft black cock
wing	barred teal flank (rolled)

Probably the best known of the teal series of flies. This fly seems more to represent a small pin fry and is a good taker of fish. We have found it most effective when the light is just beginning to fade in the evening.

Mallard & Claret

hook	10 - 14
silk	black
tail	golden-pheasant tippets
rib	fine gold wire
body	claret/crimson seal's fur
hackle	black hen
wing	bronze mallard

The best known of the Mallard series of flies. A traditional pattern and one never to be without.

Invicta

hook	10 - 14
silk	olive or brown
tail	golden-pheasant crest
rib	gold wire
body	yellow seal's fur palmered with light red game-cock
wing	hen-pheasant centre tail
beard	blue jay

Invicta

Never leave home without this fly if there is a chance of hatching sedges on the water.

Black & Peacock Spider

hook	10 - 14
silk	black
body	bronze peacock herl
hackle	3-4 turns of long fibred black hen

Note:a silver wire rib can be added if desired.

A simple fly but very effective. This fly can represent a static floating snail, a hatching dry fly or even a small nymph when tied slim. A good all-round fly and easy to tie.

Dunkeld

hook	10 - 12
silk	black
tail	small golden pheasant crest
rib	oval gold tinsel
body	flat gold tinsel
wings	brown mallard shoulder feather with jungle cock on each side

A fly of Scottish origin but much used on Northern waters. A good hatching sedge pattern.

Dunkeld

Black Gnat

hook	14 - 18
silk	black
body	black quill, tying silk or horsehair
wings	pale starling or 2 small pale-blue dun hackle tips tied flat on back
hackle	black cock or starling neck feather

Black Gnat

Although most people might consider the Black Gnat a dry fly, we have found it can also account for a good many fish when retrieved just below the surface.

Kate Maclaren

hook	10 - 12
silk	black
tail	golden pheasant topping
rib	oval silver tinsel
body	black seal's fur well picked out
body hackle	black cock hackle
hackle	red-brown cock of soft grade

A traditional Scottish loch fly by origin but its quality is being recognised more so in recent years. A fly that may produce fish when others fail.

March Brown

hook	12 - 14
silk	brown
tail	partridge tail fibres
rib	fine gold wire
body	dubbed hare's ear fur or brown seal's fur
wing	brown partridge or hen pheasant
hackle	brown partridge

March Brown (wingless)

Probably more known as a river fly than stillwater, but this is a very adaptable pattern and well worth carrying in the fly box.

Teal, Blue & Silver

hook	10 - 12
silk	black
tail	golden pheasant tippets
rib	fine silver wire
body	flat silver tinsel
wing	rolled barred teal
beard	blue dyed feather fibres

Dry Flies

G & H Sedge (Goddard and Henry)

hook	8 - 12
silk	olive green
body	spun deer hair trimmed to shape
under-body	dark green seal's fur
hackle	2 rusty dun cock hackles
antennae	quills from hackle brought forward

G. & H. Sedge

This fly has accounted for many trout and is an excellent fly if fished when natural sedges are on the water. It can be fished static or "skittered" across the surface imitating the natural.

Greenwell's Glory

hook	12 - 14
silk	primrose
body	waxed tying silk
rib	fine gold wire
hackle	light furnace hen hackle
wing	slips from a grey mallard primary feather

A traditional fly that has proved itself and has stood the test of time. It is universally used and imitates the many pond olive species.

Pond Olive

hook	12 - 16
silk	olive
rib	fine silver wire
tail	olive feather fibres
body	tying silk
hackle	soft olive hackle feather
wing	starling slips or olive dyed feather slips

A fly very much like the Greenwell's Glory but meant to represent a definite insect.

Adams

hook	12 - 16
silk	grey
tail	grizzle hackle fibres
body	blue-grey dubbed wool or fur
wings	two grizzle hackles tied up-right
hackle	red grizzle cock

If we were only allowed one dry fly to fish with it would probably be an "Adams". This fly seems to take fish on any water when dry flies are about. An excellent fly that will take brown and rainbow trout alike. We have found this fly best in the smaller sizes.

Soldier Palmer

hook	10 - 14
silk	black
tail & body	red wool
rib	gold or silver oval tinsel
body hackle	medium brown cock

We like to fish this as a dry pattern although it is just as good when fished in the surface film or just under. This fly may take fish when they are being choosy.

Hopper

hook	10 - 12
silk	as colour of fly
body	seal's fur
rib	pearly tinsel
legs	knotted pheasant tail fibres (3 per side)
hackle	dyed cock hackle to suit body colour

Hopper

A hopper can be a devastating fly when this is what the fish want. The fly seems to represent many different food forms and can be tied in many different colours ranging from black through to light ginger.

Daddy-Longlegs

hook	l/s 10
silk	brown
rib	clear nylon monofilament
body	buff feather fibre
legs	6 knotted pheasant tail fibres (3 per side)
wing	red game hackle points
thorax	as for body
hackle	red game cock

Never be without this pattern. From the beginning of autumn, when the naturals are falling on the water, the trout love them. But be prepared for some vicious takes. The fly can also be fished wet or just allowed to sink when the fish will take them on the drop.

Grey Duster

hook	12 - 16
silk	brown
body	light natural rabbit
hackle	badger cock

A dry fly that will take trout on stillwaters nationwide. Not meant to imitate any fly in particular but very useful when midges are on the water.

Grey Wulff

hook	8 - 14
silk	black
tail	natural bucktail fibres
body	grey rabbit fur or angora wool
wing	brown bucktail tied upright or split in a "v" shape
hackle	blue-dun cock

Invented by Lee Wulff around 1930, this fly has developed a universal reputation for taking trout. An excellent fly.

Hawthorn Fly

hook	10 - 12
silk	black
abdomen	black feather fibre
rib	black tying silk
thorax	black feather fibre
wings	2 white hackle-points tied in back-to-back
legs	2 fibres of swan herl dyed black, knotted twice

Meant to represent the natural fly, Bibio Marci, this is an easy fly to recognise with its thick body and elongated trailing legs. A great fly when the naturals hatch around May to June when the hawthorn blossom is out.

Buzzer Fishing

We have deliberately left these buzzer patterns until last because we feel that Buzzer fishing is almost a separate form of fishing in its own right. There are many patterns, which range from a simple loop or two of wire around a hook shank to more elaborate tyings with wing-buds; breather filaments, and all, come in a multitude of colours.

Buzzers are the pupae stage of the midge life cycle and are usually, (but not always), fished on very long leaders, (up to twenty feet or more is not uncommon). The line is cast out and either left to drift around in the breeze, or retrieved with a very slow figure of eight. Anglers must watch their leader constantly for the slightest movement, and be prepared to strike at any moment. For this reason some anglers prefer to use a bite indicator or sight bob when buzzer fishing, but as long as the fishery rules permit the use of these aids, it is entirely up to the individual, but be warned that some fisheries do not allow the use of bite indicators. A number of anglers we have met fish nothing else but buzzers and are very successful throughout the year, which shows that buzzers are very high on the trout's menu. Buzzers can be fished at all depths so you must be prepared to experiment to find the feeding depth.

It is probably worth mentioning here the bloodworm pattern. Although not a buzzer, the bloodworm is the larval stage of the chironomid midge. It lives mainly in the mud on lake beds but rises to more oxygenated water levels to replenish its own supply and at this time it is readily accepted by the trout. Best fished slow and deep, this fly can be a good taker of fish in the summer months.

Buzzer Patterns

As stated earlier, there are many different buzzer patterns, so we have included only a few of our favourites here. These are the patterns we use which may vary from the original patterns.

Shipman's Buzzer

hook	10-14
silk	orange
body	orange seal's fur or substitute
rib	silver wire
breathers	white Antron wool

Black Buzzer

hook	10-16
silk	black
body	tying silk
rib	fine silver wire
breathers	white Antron wool

Black Shipman's Buzzer

Copper Wire Buzzer

hook	10-16
silk	none
body	spaced turns of copper wire, built up at the head
over body	three coats of clear varnish

Bead Buzzer

hook	12
silk	none
body	coloured beads superglued onto the hook shank
overbody	three coats of clear varnish

Black Buzzer

C.D.C. Buzzer

Hook	12 - 14
Silk	as required body colour
Rib	fine silver wire
Thorax and breathers	a small bunch of cul de cunard feathers tied to extend over the eye of the hook

Lime Green Buzzer

Hook	10 - 14
Silk	fluorescent lime green floss
Rib	fine silver wire

Just for Starters:
Basic equipment for beginners

There are two basic ways to catch trout on our region's stillwaters, one is fly fishing, and the other is bait fishing, particularly using worms.

Rods

For fly fishing an angler needs a fly rod. An all-round rod to cope with a variety of conditions would be about three metres long and rated at number seven in the AFTM scale. This stands for American Fishing Tackle Manufacturers and is a recognised weight scale for fishing tackle. The rod then needs a fly reel, which houses the line. The reel needs to be fairly robust so it can take the knocks it may sometimes receive. Some reels have a drag system so that when a trout is hooked there is some resistance against the line as the fish runs and so tires quicker. The reel needs to house whichever fly line the angler has chosen plus about 80 to 100 yards of backing line. Most reels have spare spools available, which can be changed quickly and easily thus allowing the angler to change lines as the conditions dictate.

Lines, of which there are many, should be matched to the rating of the rod. If a rod is rated as a number seven, then the angler needs to buy line rated at seven. Probably a Double Taper floating line would be best to begin with. Double Taper means that the line is level in the middle section but tapers at each end and when one end is worn, the line can be reversed and the opposite end used, giving the line a longer life. A line like this would probably be sold or advertised as a **DT7F** indicating it is a **D**ouble **T**aper, **Seven** weight **F**loating line. The first letters being the profile of the line, the number indicating the weight, and the last letter indicating whether it **F**loats, **S**inks or is an **I**ntermediate line. There are many lines in-between, but we will only mention lines that may concern the beginner.

The tippet, or leader, is the length of nylon between the fly line and the fly itself. To begin with, the angler would probably use a leader of about the same length as the rod and with a breaking strain of around six pounds. Tapered leaders are available and droppers can be used too, but these are for the more experienced angler.

Other equipment

A landing net is necessary for fishing, although at least one water, Jubilee Lakes, provides them. This is usually to prevent any disease being transferred between fisheries. All landing nets must now be of knot-less mesh so that fish can be returned with the minimum of stress. For boat fishing, shorter nets can be used, while for bank fishing longer handled nets are preferable. A net with a point on the handle is useful when wading as this can be stuck into the lake bed next to the angler.

A pair of glasses is always advised to protect the eyes from stray flies, particularly in windy conditions. Polarised glasses are an added advantage so that the angler can see into the water for fish or signs of movement or activity.

Carrying a priest is a must to administer the last rites to the trout. This action must be carried out quickly and cleanly if the trout is not to be returned to the water.

Snips or scissors and forceps are essential equipment too. Tippets need cutting next to the fly line or fly regularly, so some sort of cutting implement is needed. Forceps are used to remove deep hooks or flies that have been swallowed well down the throat.

Clothing

Many anglers carry their essential fishing tackle and accessories in a fly fishing waistcoat. Other anglers have ordinary jackets and everything is carried in some sort of bag or box. The box, similar to those used by sea fishermen, have the advantage of being able to double up and be used as a seat when needed. A waistcoat, which is waterproof, is a good aid. The numerous pockets, of varying sizes, can carry just about everything the angler needs, apart from lunch and a hot drink. Waistcoats vary in size, colour, design and some are inflatable but obviously cost plays an important role.

Waistcoats lead into clothing generally, but the basic rule is to wear something suitable – as the scouts say "be prepared". Keep warm and always carry something that is waterproof. It is an unwritten law that if you have no waterproofs then you will be caught in the heaviest shower or storm miles from the nearest shelter. For cold weather try not to wear thick garments but instead concentrate on having more layers of clothes with a waterproof outer shell. Waders protect legs and chest waders cover any potential gaps in the middle region around the waistline. Neoprene waders are the warmest. Sometimes chest waders are banned on certain fisheries because of safety reasons as they are so high. Felt-soled waders are preferred for rock bottoms and please remember never to wear waders in a boat for obvious reasons.

Tuition

Local tuition is available from, amongst others:

Alan Page: Tel or fax: 0191 212 1023; Mobile: 07773 730210

Chris Guthrie: Tel: 01670 736 926

Don Coe: Tel: 01207 255 250

Alan and Don each hold a Salmon and Trout Angling National Instructors Course Certificate.

The Quarry

The local North-East reservoirs and private stillwaters stock a variety of trout. Each fishery has its own rules, so anglers must be able to recognise the quarry they wish to catch. The three main types of trout stocked are:

★ Rainbow trout

★ Brown trout

★ Brook trout

Some waters allow anglers to keep whatever they catch, but others insist that brown trout be returned immediately. Being able to recognise each type of trout will ensure a quick return rather than wasting precious minutes waiting for someone else to confirm your fish should be returned or not. Sin of sins: imagine walking up to the lodge, immensely proud of your catch, and asking the owner or manager to weigh your fish. Then experiencing the embarassment of being told it should have been returned and not killed.

Hopefully, this section provide a little background information and will also help anglers identify the different types of trout and so avoid problems. But if anyone is still unsure about the differences, especially between rainbow and brown trout, then most fisheries have posters or photographs mounted on the walls of the lodge somewhere to show off the size of trout that have been caught. These photographs often include the different types of fish and can be studied before commencing to fish. If in any doubt at all then please ask.

Rainbow Trout

Rainbow trout originated in north-western USA and were introduced into Britain during the latter part of the nineteenth century. Although there was some early resentment against these imports, it has now evaporated as anglers appreciate the species' fighting abilities.

Rainbows have been stocked in lakes and reservoirs throughout Britain as they are very adaptable to most waters. It has been found that these trout can tolerate higher water temperatures and lower oxygen levels than our own native brown trout.

Rainbow trout can have a phenomenal growth rate given the right conditions and are thought by some to be more disease resistant than brown trout. Some anglers believe that, because rainbows eat so much, they are easier to catch as they are more susceptible to the fly.

Some, but not all, lakes introduce "specimen" trout. These are very large fish weighing anything up to and over twenty-five pounds. To gain so much weight quickly these fish are given a diet of super rich pellets but once they are stocked into reservoirs these monsters can lose weight and condition rapidly if they are not caught within a relatively short period.

Sweethope Loughs have introduced a rainbow of over thirty pounds which when caught will break the North-East record. The fish was put into the small lough so it can only be caught from the bank, as there are no boats on this lough.

Some waters now only stock triploid rainbows. These are fish especially reared from eggs that have been treated to make them all sterile female fish. The advantage of this is that these fish never enter a spawning cycle and so never lose condition which means superb quality, hard fighting fish are available throughout the year.

How to identify Rainbow Trout.

The most easily identifying feature of these trout is the iridescent broad pink band that runs from the eye along the length of the body to the tail. Rainbows have a dark greenish-blue back that is covered with black spots, which continue into the tail and they are silver in the belly.

Brown Trout

Brown trout are indigenous to northern Europe and have been successfully introduced to many other countries throughout the world.

This type of trout needs clean, unpolluted water as they are less able to cope with adverse conditions than rainbow trout. They can be introduced into stillwaters of any size and though they will not breed, they can live quite happily for a number of years. Brown trout are more territorial than rainbows and can often be seen patrolling the margins. These trout can also "disappear" into the depths of the lakes and can then be more difficult to catch than the rainbows. They are definitely more difficult to rear than rainbows and this makes them more expensive to stock. In the larger English reservoirs, depending on the amount of available food, some large brown trout turn canni-balistic and are termed ferox trout.

How to identify Brown Trout

The main distinguishing feature of the brown trout is the presence of characteristic black and red spots, which cover the back and flanks. No spots can be seen on the tail and this is one of the main identifying differences between the brown and rainbow trout. In stillwaters these trout are mainly a dark buttery-yellow colour on the underside.

Brook Trout

Brook trout are a species of Arctic Char and originate from north-eastern USA and Canada. They were introduced into Europe around 1880 and are now stocked world-wide. Brook trout have a similar range of food to our native brown trout and the two species are often crossed to produce Tiger Trout. However, brook trout are less common in the North-East because of their slow growth rate which means they are very costly to rear and stock.

How to identify Brook Trout

The most distinguishing feature of the brook trout is the white edging to the front of the lower fins. They also have a greyish-green back with worm-like or marbled markings. Along the fish's flanks are spots that may vary from cream to greenish-yellow and may include red or blue spots too. They thrive in the peaty, acidic waters of the north and will attack a brightly coloured lure with gusto at all times of the year.

The Weather and its Effects

Weather conditions can and will affect fishing dramatically; particularly extreme conditions or sudden climatic changes. The fish, and many of the insects and water life they feed on, are very aware of atmospheric pressure change and can go off the feed a few days before it even gets here. Learning to read and understand a barometer is a useful tool in the anglers armoury.

Trout, in early spring when the water temperatures are still low, will usually be found in deeper water, feeding close to the bottom, but a prolonged warm spell may fetch them closer to the surface to feed. This also applies again in late autumn when a cold spell will send them back to deeper water.

But, as the water warms up and the season progresses, the trout will begin to feed in the shallower margins of the lake or reservoir, particularly in the early morning and the late evening.

Sun and wind also play a vital part and the ideal conditions for fishing occur after a spell of settled weather, with a slight breeze and good cloud cover being optimal. Heavy torrential rain and gusty wind are no friends to the fisherman and should be avoided like the plague and it is wiser to wait until conditions improve before casting a line. It is not impossible to catch fish in these conditions but it is a lot harder work. A bright clear sky with a burning sun can be just as bad as this usually puts the fish down to the very depths of the water. Bright sun alone will chase fish from the margins and the problem then is to find at what depth they are feeding. It is probably worth mentioning at this point that daphnia or water fleas form a very substantial part of the trout's diet and, as they move to different depths depending on light intensity, the trout will follow them.

Wind and current also have an effect on the trout inasmuch as the wind will tend to blow any surface food onto the leeward shore. The trout will follow and this is where they will feed the most. The breeze on this shore or bank will be blowing into your face, making casting more difficult, but as the fish are feeding closer in you will not need to cast as far.

Look for "wind lanes" on the water. These are corridors of calm water in the waves and occur when the wind speed is around ten miles per hour. Fish cruise up these lanes picking up insects trapped in the surface film.

If, in the evening, the wind dies off, watch for a slight ripple after a calm stretch of water near the bank. There are often trout feeding in the edge of this ripple and it can be a more productive area than the flat calm.

Hints & Tips

★ Don't throw away the little packets of silica-gel you get in electrical appliance packing – put one in your fly-box to soak up any dampness. Restore its dehumidifying properties by baking the gel in a hot oven for a few ninutes.

★ Carry a small sea-fishing swivel in your pocket and if you find you have twists in your line, simply attach the line to the swivel, and the swivel to any tree, post or nearby angler, run out your line and reel in minus twists.

★ If any barbed hooks get caught in your clothing, don't try to pull them out, the barb will stop you, but push the hook through until you can see the barb, flatten it and it will pull back through quite easily.

★ Always carry your EA rod licence in a resealable plastic bag to keep it dry.

★ Make your own fly boxes from plastic video boxes and foam rubber.

★ Always carry a whistle to attract attention if in difficulty.

★ Always keep an up to date fishing log. It will become a valuable source of information in years to come.

★ Clean lines regularly.

★ Always dampen knots in fluorocarbon line.

★ If your fly gets caught up in a tree or bush, always point your rod at it and pull the line, never try to pull it out with the rod.

★ Always wear a hat and glasses for safety.

★ Always take more warm clothes than you think you need – it's easier to have them and not need them than to need them and not have them.

★ Candle wax rubbed onto rod ferrules make it easy to take the rod apart.

Suppliers

The House of Hardy

Hardy is "the" name on most anglers' lips when they talk of ultimate fishing tackle. Here in the North-East, in the market town of Alnwick, seat of the Duke of Northumberland, is the home of " The House of Hardy". Open, and free to the public, the factory, museum and countrystore must be on every angler's route. The guided factory tours are at ten o'clock and two o'clock from Mondays to Thursdays, with only one tour on a Friday at ten o'clock. These arrangements operate except when the factory is on holiday. Numbers on the tour are limited so always pre-book by telephone (01665 510027).

Tackle manufacturers

The House of Hardy: Willowburn Trading Estate, Alnwick, Northumberland. Tel: 01665 602 771

Mustad O & Son Ltd. Tel: Wearside (0191) 586 9553

Century Glass Fibre Ltd. Tel: Washington (0191) 384 7584

Ian D. Martin Hand crafted fly rods. Tel: Darlington (01325) 240 911

Anglers Services (Hartlepool) Ltd. Tel: Durham (0191) 384 7584

Titan. Tel: Wearside (0191) 586 9553

Ultimate Fishing Supplies. Tel: Ebchester (01207) 560 931

Shipwreck Marine. Tel: Stockton (01642) 679 253

Tackle Shops and Dealers

Amble Angling Centre: 4 Newburgh Street, Amble, Northumberland. Tel: 01665 711 200

Angling, Leisure, Sport: 6-10 Bowsden Terrace, South Gosforth, Newcastle-upon-Tyne. Tel: 0191 213 1682
Http:/www.angling-leisure-sport.co.uk
alan@angling-leisure-sport.co.uk

Arkle's Angling: 3 Ravensworth Terrace, Bedlington, Northumberland. Tel:01670 828 887

Bagnall & Kirkwood Ltd: 28 Grey Street, Newcastle-upon-Tyne. Tel: 0191 232 5873

C.D. Fishing Tackle: 94b Front Street, Newbiggin-by-the-Sea, Northumberland. Tel: 01670 520 133

Game Fair Shooting & Fishing: 12 Marygate, Berwick.
Tel: 01289 305 119

John Robertson: 101 Percy Street, Newcastle-upon-Tyne.
Tel: 0191 232 2018

McDermott's Fishing Tackle Shop: 112 Station Road, Ashington, Northumberland. Tel: 01670 812 214; and 8 King Street, Blyth, Northumberland. Tel: 01670 365 980

M.R. Tackle: 14 Market Street, Hexham, Northumberland.
Tel: 01434 606 988

Temple's: 43 Ocean View, Whitley Bay, Tyne-and-Wear.
Tel: 0191 252 6017

Adams. W.P. Fishing Tackle Supercentre: 42 Duke Street, Darlington.
Tel: 01325 468 069

Aycliffe Angling Centre: 9 Simpasture Gate, Newton Aycliffe.
Tel: 01325 301 876

C.L.S. Angling: 21 North Burns, Chester-le-Street. Tel: 0191 388 2154

Catchum Tackle & Guns: 8-9 Murton Street, Sunderland.
Tel: 0191 514 0000

Fishing World: 23 Hope Street, Crook. Tel: 01388 765 077

Reid Fishing Tackle & Sports: 33 Hope Street, Crook.
Tel: 01388 763 867

Cairns Angling: Mains Forth Terrace, Hartlepool. Tel: 01429 272 581

West Auckland Country Store: 4-6 Staindrop Road, West Auckland.
Tel: 01388 833 333

Windrow Sports: 5-7 Fore Bondgate, Bishop Auckland.
Tel: 01388 603 759

Quali-Tye: 23 Medomsley Road, Consett. Tel: 01207 508 010

Turners Fishing Tackle: 25 Front Street, Sacriston.
Tel: 0191 371 1804

Anglers Choice: 53 Clive Road, Middlesbrough. Tel: 01642 899 288

Yarm Angling Association: 4 Blenavon Court, Yarm.
Tel: 01642 786 444

Organising Bodies

The Confederation of English Fly Fishers

The Confederation of English Fly Fishers (CEFF) is the recognised authority on competitive fly fishing in England. This confederation elects delegates to the International Fly Fishing Association (IFFA), and the International Federation of Sport Fly Fishing – *FIPS Mouche*. This is the authority under which the World and European championships are conducted. The I.F.F.A. is the authority for the conduct of the 'Home' internationals. England, Scotland, Wales and Ireland have competed in Loch-Style competition since 1932 (except for the war years). These internationals are bi-annually in the Spring and Autumn, while the annual River International Competitions only began in 1992.

The CEFF controls all fly fishing in England, and the country is covered by ten regional federations:

Anglia   North-West
Severn Trent   South-East
South-West   Southern
West Country   Yorkshire
South-East Anglia   Tyne and Wear

The contact person and number for our region is Peter Jobson (tel: 01670 521 272).

The Tyne and Wear region is organised by the Tyne and Wear Fly Fishing Association (TWFFA). This region covers the Northumbrian area which streches from Berwick in the north, to Teeside in the south and as far west as the Cumbrian border. Individual clubs affiliate annually to the TWFFA which currently costs £20. National eliminator competitions are organised for three types of fly fishing: Rivers; Loch Style (boat); Small Stillwater.

The fly fishing clubs that affiliated to the TWFFA are listed overleaf. Two clubs from Cumbria are also affiliated to the WFFA:

Penrith Fly Fishers (Penrith): Mr A. Dixon (01768 884 78)

Keswick Angling Association (Keswick): Mr M. Tinnion (01768 772 127)

Name of Club	Contact person	Telephone number
Ashington Kingfishers (Ashington)	Mr I.R. Fairgrieve	01670 851 281
Bedlington Otteres (Bedlington)	Mr S. Mulvay	01670 824 527
Chester le Street Angling Club	Mr G. Curry	0191 388 7072
Consett Invicta (Shotley Bridge)	Mr T. Nelson	01207 509 207
Durham Fly Dressers Guild Team Qualitye (Durham)	Mr S. Wardle	01429 836 793
Felling Gremlins (Gateshead)	Mr B. Mulholland	0191 496 9609
Ferryhill Dist. A.A. (Spennymoor)	Mr J. A. Lowry	01388 811 768
Hirst Park Trout Ticklers (Ashington)	Mr A. Young	01670 850 230
Hoy n Hope Fishers (Rowlands Gill)	Mr D. Smith	01670 817 116
Lambswood Fly Fishers (Rowlands Gill)	Mr G.Thompson	01207 543 423
North Biddick Gamefishers (Washington)	Mr A. Jenkins	0191 416 3517
Northumbrian Water Gamefishers (Pity Me)	Mr A. Baker	0191 383 2222
Northumbrian Ospreys (Ponteland)	Mr P.Davison	0191 495 2128
S. C. A. Angling Club (Prudhoe)	Mr J. Campbell	01661 836 899
Thornaby Angling Association (Thornaby)	Mr D. Speight	01642 881 694
Three Tuns Fly Fishers (Heddon on the Wall)	Mr R. Simpson	
Wansbeck Cormorants (Guide Post)	Mr N. Cowans	01670 530 244
Weardale Fly Fishers (Stanhope)	Mr S. Bissett	

CEFF competition rules

CEFF competition rules are split into different sections – general competition rules, loch style fishing rules, loch style match rules, river fishing rules and national river final match rules.

The general competition rules cover the details of tradition, betting, eligibility, disputes and complaints.

Loch style fishing rules examine flies, hooks, lines and leaders, rods, drifting, fishing zones around the boat, standing and sitting, command of the boat, drogues, respect for other anglers and electrical devices.

The loch style match rules examine the local rules, hours of fishing, species and size of fish, the weigh in, placings, boatmen and boat pairings, emergencies, finally and very importantly the safety aspects.

The English Open Small Stillwaters Championship (Airflow Clas-

sic) rules cover eligibility, local rules, hours of fishing, peg arrangements, flies, rods, nets and lines, fishing, placings and general CEFF
competition rules. It is interesting to note that the placings in this
competition are decided on the number of fish caught. A tie on the
number of fish is then resolved by the weights of the first two fish
caught. Should there still be a tie, the result is decided with the heaviest recorded fish.

The rules for river fishing and the National River Finals Match
Competition cover similar headings to the ones already quoted.

If any angler is interested in national competitions it is essential
that all the rules should be read and thoroughly understood. Copies
of the rules are available from the individual federations.

National Competitions

For many trout anglers the competition is against the fish, but some
people want to compete against others. On the national scene there
are now five main team competitions.

Firstly there is the House of Hardy International Fly Fishing
Championship. This competition is a six-man team competition
fished from boats. Entries can only be accepted from clubs or associa-
tions. The "Hardy" is open to fishermen from all over the UK and
Europe, but teams are supposed to fish the regional qualifying
competition closest to their club base. The regional heats of the
"Hardy" are held at different venues throughout the UK.

Anyone wishing to enter this competition can gain more information from: Chris Ogbourne, House of Hardy Fly Fishing, Pool
Cottages, Compton Martin, Bristol BS40 6LB. Tel/Fax: 01761 221108

A second national competition is the Peregrine Nomad UK International Team Challenge. This is a four-man team event and is open
to teams from the UK and Europe. Heats are held throughout the UK.

Anyone can fish as part of a team in this competition as there is no
need to belong to a club or an association. Teams progress into a two
day final following qualification from the heats. More information
can be gained from: John Horsey, Peregrine Nomad UK, Stanton
Wick, Pensford, Bristol BS39 4BZ. Tel/Fax: 10761 490367.
E-mail: peregrine@jhffs.demon.co.uk

A third team competition is The Association of Major Fly Fishing
Clubs. This competition is open to all clubs with at least fifty
members and is a boat fishing event. Clubs fish in leagues of six as

members and is a boat fishing event. Clubs fish in leagues of six as well as two Association Matches where all clubs fish together at the same venue. Individual anglers are restricted to three matches only. The organisers have adopted the Olympic principle, participation is more important than winning, so there are no cash or tackle prizes. The entry fee is £40 per club and information can be gained from Peter Firth, tel: 01304 611301.

A fourth competition is the "Small Stillwater Championship" (Airflow Classic). This is organised by the Confederation of English Fly Fishers (CEFF) and is an open bank fishing event. Anglers can enter as a team of three or as an individual and there is no requirement to be a member of any club or association. There are many heats, some 44 in all, but anglers may only enter one heat per year.

From the heats, some anglers qualify for one of four regional finals, and then if successful go on to fish in the national final. In this competition anglers draw for a "pegged" section of bank and then move around the lake fishing in different zones. This prevents some anglers fishing hot spots all day.

Prizes in this competition include an Airflow rod, reel, and Perpetual Trophy for the winning team. The second and third teams receive Airflow tackle prizes for each individual. The top individual angler in the competition receives the same prizes as each member of the winning team. To enter, contact Tony O'Dowd, tel: 01623 754537 or 01159 422148.

A fifth competition is called "Tightlines – Airflow Team Challenge". This new competition has prize money of £100,000 which is easily the biggest for any event on the fly fishing calendar. This prize money is based on expected levels of participation. Entrants should contact Simon Lock, Tightlines, 72/74 Wind Street, Ammanford Carms, SA18 3DR, tel: 01269 595858.

England Youth

The England Youth Section is affiliated to the CEFF. For youngsters (under seventeen) to represent England they must do well in the National Final. At this level England can enter up to two teams in the world championships. Countries that compete in these championships are England, Scotland, Ireland and Wales, the USA, Canada, Czechoslovakia, France, Norway, Denmark, Poland, Italy, Belgium and Spain.

had many successes at under seventeen level and these have included a number of North-East teenagers in recent years: Barry Nicholson from Stakeford, James Cowans from Guidepost, Chris Watson from Rothbury, Mark Lockyer from Blyth, Alistair Tait from Morpeth and Paul Parkes from Stakeford. All these teenagers have been capped by England and have a wealth of experience of fishing at the highest level.

Organisation of the Authorities for Fly Fishing Competitions

Area	Authority
World and European	FIPs Mouche
Home Internationals	International Fly Fishing Association
English National Championships	Confederation of English Fly Fishers

Individual area secretaries are listed below:

Secretaries	Area	Telephone number
Peter Jobson	Tyne and Wear	01670 521 272
Tony Curtis	Anglia	01778 344 730
Stephen Blundell	North-West	0161 440 0485
Brian Pargeter	Severn Trent	01203 325 248
Peter Wyles	South-East	01293 520 199
Jeff Loud	South-West	01179 311 364
Tom Carter	Southern	0198 061 1265
Peter Page	West Country	01364 654 395
Paul Page	Yorkshire	01457 867 294

National Youth Competitions are organised by the England Youth Fly Fishing Association. The secretary for this association is Mike Watts, tel: 01536 514 381.

River Fishing Competitions

Although this book concentrates on stillwater fishing, this very brief outline of river competition fishing may be of interest to some.

The Tyne and Wear Fly Fishing Association river eliminator competition is held at various venues depending on the number of entries received. Some years, when large numbers of anglers have entered, fishing has been on the River Tweed and its tributary, the Teviot. When lower numbers of entries are received, the competition is held locally on the River Wear.

Teviot. When lower numbers of entries are received, the competition is held locally on the River Wear.

A maximum of 32 competitors enter and each angler is appointed a controller. The competition has a catch and release policy with no fish being killed. Anglers pass any fish they catch to their controller who then measures, weighs and records each fish before carefully returning it to the water.

Winners of our regional heat eliminator then go on to fish in the national final. The top five rods from the national final fish for England, the sixth rod is reserve for the team.

Youngsters and the Future

Talking to anyone connected with fly fishing across the region, anglers, club officials, fishery managers and national representatives, everybody agrees there are not enough youngsters coming into our sport.

Northumbrian Water tries to encourage newcomers to trout fishing by putting on beginners courses at a number of their reservoirs. These courses are often over-subscribed and have successfully introduced many new people to both worm and fly fishing. Jubilee and Beamish Waters provide tuition free for youngsters (who are at least twelve), to fly fishing. This tuition is available but must be arranged in advance.

All these initiatives are most welcome, but are not providing the numbers of youngsters everyone would like to see enjoying trout fishing. We believe the answer to the problem lies in our schools. Hirst Park Middle School in Ashington, Northumberland seems to have set the example for the rest of the region or even the nation to follow. This school, with 480 nine- to thirteen-year-old pupils has 36 members enrolled in their trout fishing club, the "Trout Ticklers". One teacher decided to form the club to get pupils out of the town and into the countryside for one day each month during the trout fishing season. Another aim was to try to get both parents and children spending 'quality time' together. For this reason, no pupil can join the Trout Ticklers, without having at least one adult to supervise them. Sometimes it is a parent but some pupils fish with uncles or grandparents. Whole families often have a day out together.

It is good to see the pupils regularly catching far more fish than parents. Fishing outings have been arranged at Fontburn and Derwent Reservoirs, because both young and old have the choice of fishing by fly or worm. (These reservoirs are also the closest to school.) Youngsters, under 17, can also fish free on the supervisory adult ticket. Two youngsters under 17 may fish on an adult licence, sharing the bag limit. The Environmental Agency too, were willing to reduce the price of individual day licences if the school wished to bulk buy in advance. It is encouraging to see the positive help from these companies and agencies.

Everyone who joins the Trout Ticklers must agree to abide by the code of conduct, buy the club badge and wear it when fishing. Production of their badge (designed by pupils) at the local tackle shop McDermott's on Station Road in Ashington, gains a ten percent reduction on everything bought by club members.

The tension is always high as everyone brings their catch to the scales, pupils and adults alike. Two trophies are awarded at each outing to the pupils who catch the heaviest bag and the heaviest fish. The wardens at both reservoirs also present the winners with a free day's fishing ticket (an excellent gesture). Records are always kept and the end of season's totals result in numerous trophies being presented on a presentation night which is reported in the local press.

The club has no expenses, as all pupils travel to the fishing venues in their parents' cars and buying club badges pays for the cost of the badge production. The presentation evening tickets, for the disco, buffet and raffle, have resulted in a healthy bank balance. This money has been partially spent on fly rods, spinning rods and equipment for

Hirst Park Trout Ticklers trophy presentation night

potential beginners to try before buying their own gear. Anyone who has any unwanted gear could always donate it to the Trout Ticklers. (Tel: **01670 813 111**). One thing is certain, to run a club like this is hard work and time consuming.

We feel that we have covered the Trout Ticklers set-up in a little detail, but we do not apologise for this if it inspires any teacher or adult to begin a trout fishing club. Certainly, any advice sought from the Trout Ticklers on (01670) 813 111 will be welcomed and met with a very positive response. We must remember that, to get youngsters involved in our sport, the older generation must make the effort and take the time to teach younger people the art and enjoyment of fly fishing. After all, the youngsters of today will be the anglers of tomorrow.

Many other sports (even minority ones) are now appointing area or regional development officers, so why can't we? This all costs money, but grants are available from such bodies as Sport England, the brand name adopted by the English Sports Council as the distributor of

Scott Nellins with trophies at Grassholme *(courtesy of Northumbrian Water)*

Lottery funds to sport. At the time of writing, Sport England has made 34 grants to angling in general, totalling £1.7m, an amount which pales into insignificance compared with grants to spectator sports such as football and tennis. Even so – and despite the fact that prefer-ence is seemingly being given to large, ambitious projects – other sports do make successful applications for improved facilities that can help to train youngsters. So what is our sport doing? It is puzzling that few articles have appeared in fishing publications to promote sponsorship for the national youth team. Is it that no applications are being made? Or are the applications unsuccessful? Fly fishing needs a national development plan to help it to make successful bids, so that our up and coming national talent can gain the benefits that other sports already enjoy.

Youth success stories

Dale's Day

At the age of eleven, young Dale Davison from Ashington, showed every angler how to fish. He landed a nineteen pound seven ounce monster rainbow trout from Northumbrian Waters Fontburn Reservoir. Dale, a member of Hirst Park Middle School Trout Ticklers fishing club could not make their outing the previous day. To make up for the disappointment, the family decided to fish the following day. Dale fished with a worm on a bubble float, from the dam wall when he hooked the fish. After a long struggle, Dale had to borrow a landing net because he did not have one himself. In the process of landing his fish, the net broke under the monster's weight.

When Dale caught this fish, in May 1998, it was just one pound below the reservoir record. The senior warden, Bruce Dale, commented that the fish was definitely the biggest landed by a youngster at Fontburn and probably the biggest trout caught by such a young angler anywhere in the country.

Dale Davison with monster trout *(courtesy of Northumbrian Water)*

Lucy Coulter

Lucy started trout fishing at the age of nine. On her first ever fishing visit (to Fontburn Reservoir), Lucy, and her dad Jeff, were fishing a long way from the car park on the south bank.

All was quiet so Jeff decided to return to the car to get their food. While away, it had to happen, the line went tight and Lucy had a fight on her hands. Anglers on the far bank could hear her cries, "Dad, Dad, I need help, Dad, Dad".

A friend of the family, John Short, who was fishing near-by, came to Lucy's aid. The fish was played and played, eventually coming towards the shore. Having no landing net, John got into the water and lifted the fish out, but a final struggle saw the fish back in the shallows. Not to be defied again, John was back into the water and grabbed the fish and Lucy had her first-ever trout, which weighed in at eleven pounds and nine ounces.

When Jeff returned with the food the whole story was retold with much excitement. Lucy is now learning to fly fish and has caught and landed trout up to three and a half pounds. All family holidays must include fishing at some time.

Lucy with double-figure trout

Jimmy and Christopher Tuck

Jimmy Tuck has always fished since his father, Jimmy senior, showed him the tricks of the trade when he was a boy. Most of Jimmy's fishing, however, has been in the sea or rivers, but stillwater trout angling offers a new challenge for him.

Now Jimmy's time is divided between running a Sunday League Junior football team and his fishing. Jimmy, along with three friends, made the hour-long journey to Jubilee Lakes. The day was successful, with everyone catching fish and releasing many others.

Jimmy had promised Lorraine, his wife, that he would be back home between 5 and 5.30pm. At 4.25pm Jimmy told the party it would be the last cast of the day. Standing in front of the car park he cast his dad's caddis fly pattern along the bank-side. The caddis sank and Jimmy began his last, very slow retrieve of the day.

The line tightened and the fish took off on a long, deep run. It ran the full length of the lake along the right hand bank. Jimmy had only three turns of backing left on his reel, so he decided to follow the fish before the line ran out.

Jimmy Tuck with 20-pounder *(courtesy of Jubilee Lakes)*

Keeping the line tight, Jimmy soon got to the corner of the lake and had the fish under reasonable control. At this point the rainbow went on another run to the next corner just below the upper lake. Once more, Jimmy was off again following the fish. Gaining line back onto the reel, the fish played around in this area for a while before once again heading off back towards the car-park.

The monster was starting to tire now and eventually after almost half an hour a twenty- two pound thirteen ounce rainbow was netted by a friend. When lifting the fish out of the net the caddis fly was found in the net. Any longer in the water and the fish might have gained its freedom.

Eight weeks later, in October '99, Jimmy returned to Jubilee with his two sons, James and Christopher. Everyone caught fish but again that caddis fly that Jimmy's dad tied did the trick. Young Christopher, aged eleven, cast the caddis into the upper lake late in the afternoon. Another double could not resist the caddis and after a massive struggle young Christopher landed his first fly-caught double-figure Rainbow. The fish weighed in at fifteen pounds three ounces.

Chris Tuck and his dad *(courtesy of Jubilee Lakes)*

Christopher's fish won him the Lureflash Junior Topfish Competition in the December issue of *Trout Fisherman*. His prize was the choice of either a Lureflash Viper or Mamba fly rod. Anything that encourages youngsters like this, gets our full stamp of approval.

Christopher is keen to learn as much as possible about trout fishing, so he is now taking lessons for fly tying. Jimmy was proud of Christopher's achievement, and although Jimmy senior has now unfortunately passed away, he was probably looking down with that cheeky smile for which he was famous.

Fishing Log

On the next page, we have included four copyright-free master copies of our own fishing log because we feel it is an integral part of trout fishing to use such a log. Fishing logs of any description, are not readily available anywhere in the region. This one has the added advantage of being specifically designed for stillwater trout fishing, and means that any angler using this book will automatically have a comprehensive log ready to hand. Make copies before your fishing expeditions.

The box labelled "bank location or drift used" is for the angler to draw a simple plan of the lake fished and to mark on where they caught their fish. Alternatively, anglers can draw in the section of the bank or bay they fished in detail. Maintaining this simple log will help any angler to:

★ keep up to date, personal records of numbers of fish caught and their weights.

★ identify successful fly patterns relating to different venues, weather conditions, and the time of year.

★ help plan and prepare for future outings.

★ identify hot spots.

★ recall highlights of fishing expeditions – perhaps when stress levels become excessive, or the weather prevents fishing outings, when the cold winter nights draw in or the fireside beckons!

FISHING LOG

VENUE			DATE		
TIME	TO		BOAT		BANK
TYPE OF TICKET				COST	
WEATHER					
WIND DIRECTION			WIND SPEED		
METHOD OF FISHING					

SPECIES CAUGHT		WEIGHT	FLY	BANK LOCATION OR DRIFT USED	TIME
	1				
	2				
	3				
	4				
	5				
	6				

BAG WEIGHT	ADDITIONAL REMARKS

FISHING LOG

VENUE			DATE		
TIME	TO		BOAT		BANK
TYPE OF TICKET				COST	
WEATHER					
WIND DIRECTION			WIND SPEED		
METHOD OF FISHING					

SPECIES CAUGHT		WEIGHT	FLY	BANK LOCATION OR DRIFT USED	TIME
	1				
	2				
	3				
	4				
	5				
	6				

BAG WEIGHT	ADDITIONAL REMARKS

FISHING LOG

VENUE			DATE		
TIME	TO		BOAT	BANK	
TYPE OF TICKET				COST	
WEATHER					
WIND DIRECTION			WIND SPEED		
METHOD OF FISHING					

SPECIES CAUGHT	WEIGHT	FLY	BANK LOCATION OR DRIFT USED	TIME
1				
2				
3				
4				
5				
6				

BAG WEIGHT	ADDITIONAL REMARKS

FISHING LOG

VENUE			DATE		
TIME	TO		BOAT	BANK	
TYPE OF TICKET				COST	
WEATHER					
WIND DIRECTION			WIND SPEED		
METHOD OF FISHING					

SPECIES CAUGHT	WEIGHT	FLY	BANK LOCATION OR DRIFT USED	TIME
1				
2				
3				
4				
5				
6				

BAG WEIGHT	ADDITIONAL REMARKS

New/revised entries for future editions

Please use this form for new fisheries or tackle shops, and for changes to details included in this edition. Complete as appropriate, add any additions to reverse side and return to address at the foot of the form.

Name of fishery/tackle shop: . . . .
Contact person: . . . .
Telephone: . . . .
Address:. . . . .
. . . .
. . . .
. . . .

For fisheries:
Size:. . . . .
Method (fly/worm/both):. . . . .
Species:. . . . .
Season: . . . .
. . . .
Fishing times (daily): . . . .
Type of ticket(s):. . . . .
. . . .
Price(s): . . . .
. . . .
. . . .
Disabled facilities:. . . . .
. . . .
Other facilities: . . . .
Troutmasters water? Yes/No
Bank?. . . . .
Boat? . . . .
No of boats . . . .
Max: no of rods per day . . . .

Please return to:
Bob Smith, The Avenue, Loansdene, Morpeth NE61 2DF.

Also from Sigma Leisure:

ANGLING DAYS

Jack Bevan

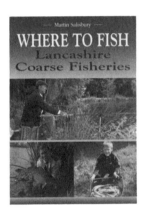

Halcyon days are recalled for all lovers of watery ways in this absorbing personal memoire. Jack Bevan shares the joys of his angling successes and humorously relives the disappointments, at the same time as he relishes the diverse natural backdrop of his angling excursions: the peaceful Yorkshire Dales, the magnificent Italian Alps, a sleepy brook in Shropshire or a clear stream in picturesque Dorset. There is an abundant supply of expertise to help the beginner and satisfy the experienced angler. All of the delights of angling are here, from visiting tackle shops and indulging in flights of fancy about success in the following season to enjoying a river idyll on a wonderful May morning. *£7.95*

WHERE TO FISH - Lancashire Coarse Fisheries

Martin Salisbury

Endorsed by Martin James, presenter of BBC Radio Lancashire's "From the Water's Edge", this book is the definitive guide to angling in Lancashire - from places on your doorstep to those you've never heard of! Covering 113 fisheries - including stillwaters, rivers and canals, and of species, rules, tickets, costs and access for each fishery. Nearby amenities are also featured - accommodation, tackle shops and local places to visit to make your day complete. *£6.95*

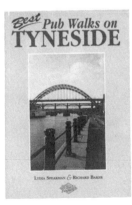

BEST PUB WALKS ON TYNESIDE

Lydia Speakman & Richard Baker

The walks are on both sides of the Tyne – alongside, over and even under it! The routes pass through a surprising variety of countryside, often using the network of old waggonways and disused railways. The strong historical flavour provides a real insight into the history of the North East. All the walks are designed to be accessible by public transport and many use the Tyne & Wear Metro System, ensuring that walkers will be able to visit the many excellent pubs described without having to worry about the drive home. *£6.95*

BEST TEA SHOP WALKS IN NORTHUMBRIA
Stephen Rickerby

Good fresh northern air and a decent northern tea to follow! These 21 varied walks in county Durham from the Tees to within 4 miles of the Scottish border each begin and end at a tea shop of character and interest. The walks vary from 2 to a little over 5 miles in length and include careful directions (with a map) for a leisurely ramble in the open air. Countryside settings are chosen for the most part - by peaceful rivers, in the hills, among the woods and along the shore - with an occasional more urban foray where history or heritage demands. *£6.95*

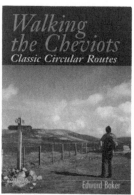

WALKING THE CHEVIOTS - Classic Circular Routes
Edward Baker

This is one of the few guides to a true wilderness area, written by an experienced author who has lived in the Cheviots all his life. Nearly 50 walks, from 2 to 14 miles. "... a must for the Cheviot walker, whether experienced in the area or a visitor eager to explore this unique range of northern hills" - RAMBLING TODAY. *£7.95*

WALKS IN THE SECRET KINGDOM: North Northumberland
Edward Baker

Covering the area between the River Aln to the South and the Scottish Border to the North, from the Cheviot Hills in the West to the North Sea in the East, this book explores a region long-neglected. The easy-to-follow routes can be linked together giving you endless walking opportunities. They are orientated towards families and tourists, suggesting places to visit to extend the day's walking, and details of local food available. The countryside is varied and dramatic, encompassing an Area of Outstanding Natural Beauty, rolling hills, rough moors, golden beaches and ancient woodlands. *£7.95*

All of our books are available through booksellers. In case of difficulty, or for a free catalogue, please contact: SIGMA LEISURE, 1 SOUTH OAK LANE, WILMSLOW, CHESHIRE SK9 6AR. Tel: 01625-531035 Fax: 01625-536800. E-mail: info@sigmapress.co.uk Web site: http//www.sigmapress.co.uk MASTERCARD and VISA orders welcome.